Spiritual
EMERGENCY

Heaven Hell

REV. ERNEST ADDO

Published 2016 by Little Books Publications, United Kingdom

First Printing 2016

Email Ernest Addo:

ernest.addo1@yahoo.com

Find out more about Ernest Addo at:

www.facebook.com/LivingJesusTabernacle

ISBN: 978-0-9932250-5-5

Printed by College Hill Press

DEDICATION

I dedicate this book specifically to all those who are passionate in seeing the Great Commission fulfilled. May the Lord give you the anointing and the grace to win the lost at all cost.

CONTENTS

Chapter 1

I AM NOT ASHAMED

There is only one way by which mankind shall be saved. It is through the miraculous power that changes lives and that is through the preaching of the gospel of Jesus Christ. Apostle Paul boldly declared that he is not ashamed of the preaching, speaking and proclamation of God's word. He openly said that he is not ashamed to be a Christian. He enjoyed witnessing and preaching to people about Jesus.

For I am not ashamed of the gospel of Christ: for it is the power of God unto salvation to every one that believeth; to the Jew first, and also to the Greek.

For therein is the righteousness of God revealed from faith to faith: as it is written, The just shall live by faith.
                                          Romans 1:16-17

Salvation is a spiritual emergency and we cannot be reluctant about it. Salvation means *"to rescue into safety"* and *"to deliver from danger."* It is an emergency. That is why Christians cannot keep silent. We must shout it from the roof tops. We must testify about Jesus and His coming to every tribe, every tongue, every kindred and every nation. We must desperately fulfil the Great Commission and preach the Gospel of Christ to the entire world. This is the core, the central and the most important duty of everyone who becomes born again.

Go ye therefore, and teach all nations, baptizing them in the name of the Father, and of the Son, and of the Holy Ghost:

Teaching them to observe all things whatsoever I have commanded you: and, lo, I am with you alway, even unto the end of the world. Amen.
                                          Matthew 28:19-20

But sadly, most Christians are even ashamed to be called Christians, let alone to preach the word of

God. Some are born again Christians and yet none of their friends, families, relatives and colleagues are aware of their experience in Jesus. They hide their Bibles in their bags because they are ashamed to carry it. This is not true Christianity. Perhaps you are not saved that is why you hide your Christianity. I encourage you to never hide your new found life in Jesus if you are truly born again! Do not be ashamed of Him because He is your Lord and Saviour. David said in Psalm 40, *"I have preached your righteousness in the great congregation" and "I have not concealed thy loving kindness."* He also said that he shall speak God's word *"before kings and will not be ashamed."*

I have preached righteousness in the great congregation: lo, I have not refrained my lips, O LORD, thou knowest.

I have not hid thy righteousness within my heart; I have declared thy faithfulness and thy salvation: I have not concealed thy lovingkindness and thy truth from the great congregation.

Psalm 40:9-10

I will speak of thy testimonies also before kings, and will not be ashamed.

Psalm 119:46

There is a danger in being ashamed of Jesus and not preaching to others about Jesus. There is a danger in hiding your Christianity because it can cost you your place in heaven. Jesus said;

Whosoever therefore shall be ashamed of me and of my words in this adulterous and sinful generation; of him also shall the Son of man be ashamed, when he cometh in the glory of his Father with the holy angels.

Mark 8:38

We must be conscious of witnessing to others. We must attach great importance and seriousness to it. People are dying every minute and men and women are dropping down to hell every second. God did not create hell for any of His children or even for the world.

Hell was made for Satan and his people and no-one else. We must propagate the gospel in order to rescue men from going down into the pit of hell. Salvation is such a precious gift from the Lord. Nothing can be compared to the gift of salvation. All that is in the world; the money, the houses and anything else you can think about, cannot match up to the value of salvation. One soul is more valuable and precious in the sight of God than everything in this world.

For what shall it profit a man, if he shall gain the whole world, and lose his own soul? Or what shall a man give in exchange for his soul?

Mark 8:36-37

Father, I ask You to give me the
burden for the lost.
I ask You blessed Holy Spirit to put
in me an unquenchable desire, hunger
and fire to see the lost saved.
Lord Jesus, if you can use anything,
please use me.
Holy Spirit, possess me and use me.
In the name of Jesus, I pray. Amen

Chapter 2

THERE IS AN EMERGENCY

E very human being you meet is walking on a path that leads to a destination. There are only two destinations that human beings go to when they die. They either go to heaven or to hell. The word of God says that *"wide is the gate and broad is the way that leads to destruction."* Sadly, many are already walking on this broad road and have chosen to go to hell. We must see this as an emergency and lead them to Jesus Christ.

Enter ye in at the strait gate: for wide is the gate, and broad is the way, that leadeth to destruction, and many there be which go in thereat:

Because strait is the gate, and narrow is the way, which leadeth unto life, and few there be that find it.
Matthew 7:13-14

Many are living in sin, many are following the world and many are evil and doing a lot of wicked things. If they knew the dangers of hell, they would surely repent of their sins and turn to Christ. It is our duty to tell them as a matter of urgency. We must tell them in our homes, tell them on the streets and in the corners, tell them at school and at work, tell them at parties and at weddings, tell them at celebrations and at meetings, tell them at the open places and in the secret places, tell them in the markets and tell them at the shops. It is a spiritual emergency.

We must rescue the perishing speedily. We must make witnessing Jesus to others our daily bread. Let it be something that you do every day. Let it be your daily routine because every person you meet is a candidate for heaven or hell. We all know that everyone will die one day. Even without an explanation from the Bible, the natural man can tell that we do not live forever. The days, the months and the years of man are determined. The word of God states in the book of Job that man's days are determined and appointed and he cannot exceed them.

Seeing his days are determined, the number of his months are with thee, thou hast appointed his bounds that he cannot pass.

Job 14:5

The word of God further emphasises that no man can say "I will not die" because no man has the power to retain his spirit at the time of death.

There is no man that hath power over the spirit to retain the spirit; neither hath he power in the day of death: and there is no discharge in that war; neither shall wickedness deliver those that are given to it.

Ecclesiastes 8:8

The word of God also says that every man shall see death and no man has the power to deliver his soul from the grave.

What man is he that liveth, and shall not see death? shall he deliver his soul from the hand of the grave? Selah.

Psalm 89:48

We were made out of dust and we shall turn to dust again.

All go unto one place; all are of the dust, and all turn to dust again.
Ecclesiastes 3:20

The writer of Hebrews explains that man has a divine appointment. No one can escape this appointment and it happens only once. This is the appointment of death which is awaiting every creature, both man and animals alike.

And as it is appointed unto men once to die, but after this the judgment:
Hebrews 9:27

It is a spiritual emergency to proclaim the gospel to every creature because no one knows their own time of death. This is the scariest thing.

If a man knows the time he will die, he will repent and make himself ready for heaven. But death happens suddenly and it happens once in the life of every human being. If the owner of a house knows when the thief will come to steal goods from his house, he will arm himself and wait for that unfortunate thief. Just as the thief comes to steal unannounced, so death comes unannounced. The Bible declares that no man knows his time of death. Even animals do not know their time of death.

For man also knoweth not his time: as the fishes that are taken in an evil net, and as the birds that are caught in the snare; so are the sons of men snared in an evil time, when it falleth suddenly upon them.

Ecclesiastes 9:12

You see, you cannot repent after you are dead. This is because there is no time for repentance as judgement comes quickly to those who die.

And as it is appointed unto men once to die, but after this the judgment:

Hebrews 9:27

There is no such thing as purgatory. The devil has been able to deceive people that they can repent and go to heaven after they are dead but this is not true. Purgatory does not exist. There are only two places that exist after death; heaven or hell. When people die in their sins they can no longer repent. No amount of prayers that is said on earth for you can change the mind of God about His judgement. In other words, once a person dies in his or her sins and does not repent, there is no more hope.

When I say unto the wicked, Thou shalt surely die; and thou givest him not warning, nor speakest to warn the wicked from his wicked way, to save his life; the same wicked man shall die in his iniquity; but his blood will I require at thine hand.

Yet if thou warn the wicked, and he turn not from his wickedness, nor from his wicked way, he shall die in his iniquity; but thou hast delivered thy soul.

Again, When a righteous man doth turn from his righteousness, and commit iniquity, and I lay a stumblingblock before him, he shall die: because thou hast not given him warning, he shall die in his sin, and his righteousness which he hath done shall not be remembered; but his blood will I require at thine hand.

Nevertheless if thou warn the righteous man, that the righteous sin not, and he doth not sin, he shall surely live, because he is warned; also thou hast delivered thy soul.

Ezekiel 3:18-21

You may have the ability to repent and even have a change of heart once you are dead but the Lord will never change His mind about the judgment you have received. The rich man in Luke chapter 16 soon realised that hell was not a nice place but he was not given a chance to repent or change his mind. In other words, repentance in hell is unacceptable and does not count. Read it for yourself.

There was a certain rich man, which was clothed in purple and fine linen, and fared sumptuously every day:

And there was a certain beggar named Lazarus, which was laid at his gate, full of sores,

And desiring to be fed with the crumbs which fell from the rich man's table: moreover the dogs came and licked his sores.

And it came to pass, that the beggar died, and was carried by the angels into Abraham's bosom: the rich man also died, and was buried;

And in hell he lift up his eyes, being in torments, and seeth Abraham afar off, and Lazarus in his bosom.

And he cried and said, Father Abraham, have mercy on me, and send Lazarus, that he may dip the tip of his finger in water, and cool my tongue; for I am tormented in this flame.

But Abraham said, Son, remember that thou in thy lifetime receivedst thy good things, and likewise

Lazarus evil things: but now he is comforted, and thou art tormented.

And beside all this, between us and you there is a great gulf fixed: so that they which would pass from hence to you cannot; neither can they pass to us, that would come from thence.

Then he said, I pray thee therefore, father, that thou wouldest send him to my father's house:

For I have five brethren; that he may testify unto them, lest they also come into this place of torment.

Abraham saith unto him, They have Moses and the prophets; let them hear them.

And he said, Nay, father Abraham: but if one went unto them from the dead, they will repent.

And he said unto him, If they hear not Moses and the prophets, neither will they be persuaded, though one rose from the dead.

Luke 16:19-31

⤜⤏

Chapter 3

JUDGMENT

Whether we like it or not, judgment awaits every person on earth. We must each face our Creator after death. Judgment will be read to us based on whether we accepted Jesus Christ as our Lord or not. This judgment is to determine where our final destination will be once we depart from the earth.

And as it is appointed unto men once to die, but after this the judgment:

Hebrews 9:27

For we must all appear before the judgment seat of Christ; that every one may receive the things done in his body, according to that he hath done, whether it be good or bad.

2 Corinthians 5:10

For God shall bring every work into judgment, with every secret thing, whether it be good, or whether it be evil.

Ecclesiastes 12:14

TWO TYPES OF JUDGEMENT

We tend to live our lives making plans for only the 70 or 80 years of our short lives and never preparing for eternity. But I want you to know that it is better to prepare for eternity where judgement pronounced is forever. You see, on earth, even when a person is sentenced to life imprisonment, some are still able to get their judgement reversed. This is not so on the other side of the world. There are two types of judgements that await every man after death. Once you receive this judgement after death, it is irreversible and it is forever. Prepare yourself well to face this judgement with victory.

First Judgement - Judgment to Hell or Heaven

There are two judgments that will take place after death. The first judgement comes immediately after death where man is thrust quickly into heaven or hell. This makes it impossible to have enough time for repentance. This is why I said earlier that the doctrine of purgatory is nonsense. There is no time to change your mind because the first judgment is so quick.

Let death seize upon them, and let them go down quick into hell: for wickedness is in their dwellings, and among them.

Psalm 55:15

And thou, Capernaum, which art exalted to heaven, shalt be thrust down to hell.

Luke 10:15

But I will forewarn you whom ye shall fear: Fear him, which after he hath killed hath power to cast into hell; yea, I say unto you, Fear him.

Luke 12:5

The above scriptures describe the manner of the first judgment. It uses words like *"thrust into hell"*, *"quick into hell"* and *"cast into hell."* In other words, the souls that die in their sins are thrust into hell, descend quickly into hell and are cast into hell as soon as they die. On the other hand, those who sincerely served the Lord are thrust quickly into heaven as soon as they die. A pastor once told of his real life story of when the Lord took him to hell. According to this pastor, his wife had wronged him and he never found room in his heart to forgive the wife. He then had an accident and became unconscious. While unconscious, the Lord took him to hell and told him that, if he was to be judged in that instant he would go to hell.

He was very surprised because he had served God all his life. But what was really astonishing was what he saw whilst in hell. He said while he was talking to the Lord in hell, people were dropping at top speed into hell every second. He was amazed at the amount of people that were being cast into hell every second. This confirms the fact that the first judgement is very quick and there is no room for repentance. The first judgement is necessary because the wicked who die are made to go to hell to wait for the second judgment.

Second Judgment - Judgment into the Lake of Fire

For if God spared not the angels that sinned, but cast them down to hell, and delivered them into chains of darkness, to be reserved unto judgment.

2 Peter 2:4

Hell is a waiting place for sinners and the scripture above confirms this. It makes it clear that, although the angels were cast down to hell, they were reserved there until judgment. This is because even though they have been cast down to hell, there is a further judgment where those who disobeyed the Father will be further cast down into the lake of fire. This second judgment will take place when the Son of man, who is Jesus, comes in His glory to judge both those who are alive and those who are dead.

Who shall give account to him that is ready to judge the quick and the dead.

1 Peter 4:5

When the Son of man shall come in his glory, and all the holy angels with him, then shall he sit upon the throne of his glory:

And before him shall be gathered all nations: and he shall separate them one from another, as a shepherd divideth his sheep from the goats:
And he shall set the sheep on his right hand, but the goats on the left.

Then shall the King say unto them on his right hand, Come, ye blessed of my Father, inherit the kingdom prepared for you from the foundation of the world:

For I was an hungred, and ye gave me meat: I was thirsty, and ye gave me drink: I was a stranger, and ye took me in:

Naked, and ye clothed me: I was sick, and ye visited me: I was in prison, and ye came unto me.

Then shall the righteous answer him, saying, Lord, when saw we thee an hungred, and fed thee? or thirsty, and gave thee drink?

When saw we thee a stranger, and took thee in? or naked, and clothed thee?

Or when saw we thee sick, or in prison, and came unto thee?

And the King shall answer and say unto them, Verily I say unto you, Inasmuch as ye have done it unto one of the least of these my brethren, ye have done it unto me.

Then shall he say also unto them on the left hand, Depart from me, ye cursed, into everlasting fire, prepared for the devil and his angels:

For I was an hungred, and ye gave me no meat: I was thirsty, and ye gave me no drink:
I was a stranger, and ye took me not in: naked, and ye clothed me not: sick, and in prison, and ye visited me not.

Then shall they also answer him, saying, Lord, when saw we thee an hungred, or athirst, or a stranger, or naked, or sick, or in prison, and did not minister unto thee?

Then shall he answer them, saying, Verily I say unto you, In asmuch as ye did it not to one of the least of these, ye did it not to me.

And these shall go away into everlasting punishment: but the righteous into life eternal.

Matthew 25:31-46

This second judgment will ensure that those who are already waiting in hell, as well as those who accept the mark of the beast while alive, are cast into the lake of fire. The lake of fire is positioned right below hell. Here the fire which is already in hell changes into a lake like a volcano. The book of Revelation describes this judgment.

And the beast was taken, and with him the false prophet that wrought miracles before him, with which he deceived them that had received the mark of the beast, and them that worshipped his image. These both were cast alive into a lake of fire burning with brimstone.

Revelation 19:20

And the devil that deceived them was cast into the lake of fire and brimstone, where the beast and the false prophet are, and shall be tormented day and night for ever and ever.

And I saw a great white throne, and him that sat on it, from whose face the earth and the heaven fled away; and there was found no place for them.

And I saw the dead, small and great, stand before God; and the books were opened: and another book was opened, which is the book of life: and the dead were judged out of those things which were written in the books, according to their works.

And the sea gave up the dead which were in it; and death and hell delivered up the dead which were in them: and they were judged every man according to their works.

And death and hell were cast into the lake of fire. This is the second death.

And whosoever was not found written in the book of life was cast into the lake of fire.

Revelation 20:10-15

꧁꧂

Chapter 4

PARADISE

The word "paradise" comes from the Greek word "paradeisos" which means *"a park, a pleasure-ground, a forest, an orchard."* Paradise is likened to the Garden of Eden.

And one of the malefactors which were hanged railed on him, saying, If thou be Christ, save thyself and us.

But the other answering rebuked him, saying, Dost not thou fear God, seeing thou art in the same condemnation?

And we indeed justly; for we receive the due reward of our deeds: but this man hath done nothing amiss.

And he said unto Jesus, Lord, remember me when thou comest into thy kingdom.

And Jesus said unto him, Verily I say unto thee, To day shalt thou be with me in paradise.

Luke 23:39-43

How that he was caught up into paradise, and heard unspeakable words, which it is not lawful for a man to utter.

2 Corinthians 12:4

He that hath an ear, let him hear what the Spirit saith unto the churches; To him that overcometh will I give to eat of the tree of life, which is in the midst of the paradise of God.

Revelation 2:7

The Hebrew word for paradise is *"Pardec"* which is translated as meaning *"orchard"* or *"forest."* This word can be found in the following scriptures.

Thy plants are an orchard of pomegranates, with pleasant fruits; camphire, with spikenard.

Song of Solomon 4:13

I made me gardens and orchards, and I planted trees in

them of all kind of fruits:

Ecclesiastes 2:5

And a letter unto Asaph the keeper of the king's forest, that he may give me timber to make beams for the gates of the palace which appertained to the house, and for the wall of the city, and for the house that I shall enter into. And the king granted me, according to the good hand of my God upon me.

Nehemiah 2:8

Paradise in the Lower Part of the Earth

There are two paradises that exist and they are found in two different locations. One can be found in the lower part of the earth and other paradise can be found in heaven. The word of God says in Ephesians chapter 4 that Jesus descended into the lower part of the earth. When Jesus died, He went into the lower part of the earth and spent three days and three nights. What did Jesus go and do there?

Wherefore he saith, When he ascended up on high, he led captivity captive, and gave gifts unto men.

(Now that he ascended, what is it but that he also descended first into the lower parts of the earth?

He that descended is the same also that ascended up far above all heavens, that he might fill all things.)
Ephesians 4:8-10

Jesus went into the lower part of the earth called paradise but not into hell. Therefore, the lower part of the earth does not consist only of hell but also paradise.

In Luke 16:22, the Bible uses the phrase *"Abraham's bosom"* to refer to paradise.

And it came to pass, that the beggar died, and was carried by the angels into Abraham's bosom: the rich man also died, and was buried;
Luke 16:22

This paradise was in close proximity to hell. That is why the rich man could still see Lazarus and Father Abraham.

And in hell he lift up his eyes, being in torments, and seeth Abraham afar off, and Lazarus in his bosom.
Luke 16:23

There was a great gap or gulf between the rich man and Lazarus but the rich man could still see Lazarus afar off. The rich man was in hell but Lazarus being in Abraham's bosom was in paradise, together with Father Abraham. The rich man could see paradise but he could not go there because there was a great gap between them. You see, the paradise located in the lower part of the earth is the place where the old saints or Christians used to go and they were held there against their will by the devil. The devil held them in captivity. That is why the word of God mentions in Ephesians chapter 4 that Jesus ascended and led captivity captive.

Wherefore he saith, When he ascended up on high, he led captivity captive, and gave gifts unto men.

(Now that he ascended, what is it but that he also descended first into the lower parts of the earth?
Ephesians 4:8-9

Forasmuch then as the children are partakers of flesh and blood, he also himself likewise took part of the same; that through death he might destroy him that had the power of death, that is, the devil;

And deliver them who through fear of death were all their lifetime subject to bondage.
Hebrews 2:14-15

When Jesus died, He went to paradise which is in the lower part of the earth and defeated Satan. He overpowered Satan and his cohorts and He freed the old saints that were kept captive. In Matthew 27:50-53, the Bible says that when Jesus died the graves were opened. Many bodies of the souls which were in those graves arose and went into the holy city and were seen by many people. These were the saints that had been held in captivity by the devil in paradise. But Jesus freed them and resurrected with them when He rose up from the dead on the third day.

Jesus, when he had cried again with a loud voice, yielded up the ghost.

And, behold, the veil of the temple was rent in twain from the top to the bottom; and the earth did quake, and the rocks rent;

And the graves were opened; and many bodies of the saints which slept arose,

And came out of the graves after his resurrection, and went into the holy city, and appeared unto many.
                                                    Matthew 27:50-53

Jesus triumphed over Satan and his demons in paradise and led captivity captive. He made a public show over them. He has the power over the grave because even the grave could not hold Him captive.

Blotting out the handwriting of ordinances that was against us, which was contrary to us, and took it out of the way, nailing it to his cross;

And having spoiled principalities and powers, he made a shew of them openly, triumphing over them in it.

Colossians 2:14-15

Do you remember the two thieves that were crucified with the Lord on the cross? Remember that Jesus said to one of them, *"today you shall be with me in paradise."* We learnt earlier that when Jesus died, He descended into the lower part of the earth. He went to paradise, which is in the lower part of the earth, with the thief on the cross.

And one of the malefactors which were hanged railed on him, saying, If thou be Christ, save thyself and us.

But the other answering rebuked him, saying, Dost not thou fear God, seeing thou art in the same condemnation?

And we indeed justly; for we receive the due reward of our deeds: but this man hath done nothing amiss.

And he said unto Jesus, Lord, remember me when thou comest into thy kingdom.

And Jesus said unto him, Verily I say unto thee, To day shalt thou be with me in paradise.

Luke 23:39-43

Paradise in Heaven

He that hath an ear let him hear what the Spirit saith unto the churches; To him that overcometh will I give to eat of the tree of life, which is in the midst of the paradise of God.

Revelation 2:7

The paradise of God mentioned in the scripture above is the paradise in the midst of heaven. This paradise itself is not heaven but a part of heaven which is similar to a garden, like the Garden of Eden. The Garden of Eden in the book of Genesis was a kind of paradise on the earth and it has similar attributes to the paradise of heaven. Notice that the tree of life in the paradise of God was in the same location, in the midst of the garden, just like in Genesis 2:9,10.

And out of the ground made the LORD God to grow every tree that is pleasant to the sight, and good for food; the tree of life also in the midst of the garden, and the tree of knowledge of good and evil.

And a river went out of Eden to water the garden; and from thence it was parted, and became into four heads.

Genesis 2:9-10

Revelation 22:1-3 describes the paradise of God in detail.

And he shewed me a pure river of water of life, clear as crystal, proceeding out of the throne of God and of the Lamb.

In the midst of the street of it, and on either side of the river, was there the tree of life, which bare twelve manner of fruits, and yielded her fruit every month: and the leaves of the tree were for the healing of the nations.

And there shall be no more curse: but the throne of God and of the Lamb shall be in it; and his servants shall serve him.

Revelation 22:1-3

Those whom the Lord has given the opportunity to see heaven often describe a garden where even the plants are alive and can speak and worship the Lord. This is a beautiful paradise where I want to be and I long to be there worshiping my Maker. Apostle Paul was caught up into the paradise of God. According to Paul, he heard unspeakable words and he encountered a great man of such that he will glory.

And I knew such a man, (whether in the body, or out of the body, I cannot tell: God knoweth;)

How that he was caught up into paradise, and heard unspeakable words, which it is not lawful for a man to utter.

Of such an one will I glory: yet of myself I will not glory, but in mine infirmities.

2 Corinthians 12:3-5

෧ඏ

Chapter 5

HELL

Some people do not believe that hell is an actual place that exists. I am here to announce to you that hell is a very real and terrible place. "Shehole" is the Hebrew word for hell and it is translated as *"hades"* or *"the world of the dead."* The Greek word for hell is also called "hades" and is translated as *"a place of departed souls"* or more simply *"the grave."* People often say "if God is so loving, how can He create a horrible place called hell for mankind?" But wait a minute. Think about the rulers of this world. They are wise enough to create a place called prison for people who are deemed unfit to live in society due to their wicked nature. Why will God not have a place called hell for disobedient, wicked and evil people who enjoy doing evil all their lifetime? It may interest you to know that God has two sides. One side is love and mercy and the other side is judgment. God is righteous and just and His judgments are true and just. God did not create hell for mankind, He created it for Satan and his demons that work with him.

Then shall he say also unto them on the left hand, Depart from me, ye cursed, into everlasting fire, prepared for the devil and his angels:

Matthew 25:41

Therefore, any man who finds himself in hell went there by choice. I have witnessed to people who have impudently replied that they want to go to hell and that they couldn't care less about hell. It is a deliberate choice made by those who go to hell.

God does not drag people to hell or heaven. He has given every man a will and a choice to do whatever they wish to do with their lives. If you choose to go to hell, you cannot blame God for it. The wish of the Lord is that all men shall be saved. In fact, He has made a wonderful provision for all men to be saved, through His dear son Jesus Christ.

Who will have all men to be saved, and to come unto the knowledge of the truth.

1 Timothy 2:4

For God so loved the world, that he gave his only begotten Son, that whosoever believeth in him should not perish, but have everlasting life.

For God sent not his Son into the world to condemn the world; but that the world through him might be saved.
John 3:16-17

God demonstrated His great love toward us even while we were still evil and wicked. While we were still sinning, He sent His only son Jesus to come into this world to pay the penalty of sin for us. Jesus came to die for sinners like us. He came to die for an ungodly world. Think about it. People are not willing to die for a good person let alone to die for a sinner. But God chose to sacrifice His precious son for sinners that they might be saved.

But God commendeth his love toward us, in that, while we were yet sinners, Christ died for us.
Romans 5:8

He became sin that we might be free from sin and not enter into hell.

For he hath made him to be sin for us, who knew no sin; that we might be made the righteousness of God in him.
2 Corinthians 5:21

What manner of love is this that our Father in heaven has bestowed on us? Make a decision right now that you shall not go to hell because that is not the plan of your Father in heaven for you. Decide today to accept Jesus as your Lord and Saviour. Decide today, not just to escape hell but also to experience the love of your Father in heaven. God longs to see you in heaven and have a sweet fellowship with you.

Location of Hell

Both the Old and the New Testament give the location of hell as being beneath the earth. Jesus himself gave the location of hell when He told the city of Capernaum that they will be brought down to hell if they did not repent.

And thou, Capernaum, which art exalted unto heaven, shalt be brought down to hell: for if the mighty works, which have been done in thee, had been done in Sodom, it would have remained until this day.

Matthew 11:23

In Luke chapter 16, both the rich man and the beggar Lazarus died and were buried. Notice that suddenly, the rich man was in hell and Lazarus was in Abraham's bosom, having a welcome reception with angels. As I studied these scriptures, the Holy Ghost whispered to me and said, "the grave is the gateway to hell." That is why one of the meanings of hell is the grave. Now, in the olden days, hell was in close proximity to paradise. This paradise referred to the paradise under the earth where the Old Testament saints were kept against their will by the devil. Both the rich man and Lazarus were buried under the earth. Yet one of them went to hell and the other went to paradise, also known as Abraham's bosom. This confirms the fact that the gateway to hell is the grave. Every graveyard is therefore a gate to hell which is beneath the earth. However, those who served the Lord while on earth, though they are buried, still find themselves in heaven.   Read the passage below.

And it came to pass, that the beggar died, and was carried by the angels into Abraham's bosom: the rich man also died, and was buried;

And in hell he lift up his eyes, being in torments, and seeth Abraham afar off, and Lazarus in his bosom.
Luke 16:22-23

I remember reading about hell in Rev. Kenneth E Hagin's book called I Believe in Visions. Rev. Hagin gave an account of dying and seeing himself being dragged down to hell. According to him, he was not saved then and that is the reason why he found himself there.

The Bible contains numerous scriptures concerning hell. I will demonstrate that hell is beneath the earth using several scriptures from the word of God. Proverbs 15:24 gives the exact location of hell. It states that the way of life is above to the wise that he may depart from hell beneath.

The way of life is above to the wise, that he may depart from hell beneath.

Proverbs 15:24

In the same book of Proverbs, in Proverbs 7:27, the strange woman's house is described as the way to hell going down to the chambers of death.

Her house is the way to hell, going down to the chambers of death.

Proverbs 7:27

Psalm 55:15 tells us that the dead go down quickly into hell.

Let death seize upon them, and let them go down quick into hell: for wickedness is in their dwellings, and among them.

Psalm 55:15

The following scriptures also gives the location of hell as being under the earth.

Yet thou shalt be brought down to hell, to the sides of the pit.

Isaiah 14:15

I made the nations to shake at the sound of his fall, when I cast him down to hell with them that descend into the pit: and all the trees of Eden, the choice and best of Lebanon, all that drink water, shall be comforted in the nether parts of the earth.

They also went down into hell with him unto them that be slain with the sword; and they that were his arm, that dwelt under his shadow in the midst of the heathen.

Ezekiel 31:16-17

And they shall not lie with the mighty that are fallen of the uncircumcised, which are gone down to hell with their weapons of war: and they have laid their swords under their heads, but their iniquities shall be upon their bones, though they were the terror of the mighty in the land of the living.

Ezekiel 32:27

Though they dig into hell, thence shall mine hand take them; though they climb up to heaven, thence will I bring them down:

Amos 9:2

For great is thy mercy toward me: and thou hast delivered my soul from the lowest hell.

Psalm 86:13

For a fire is kindled in mine anger, and shall burn unto the lowest hell, and shall consume the earth with her increase, and set on fire the foundations of the mountains.

Deuteronomy 32:22

But he knoweth not that the dead are there; and that her guests are in the depths of hell.

Proverbs 9:18

It is as high as heaven; what canst thou do? deeper than hell; what canst thou know?

Job 11:8

Description of Hell

The Bible gives a vivid description of hell that emphasises that it is a city in the underworld. The prisons of the world are an exact copy of hell.

Most Hollywood movies that depict hell also show something that is similar to it. The word of God says in Isaiah 5:14 that hell has enlarged itself and opened its mouth without measure. For that reason, many can go in at the same time. Think about the millions of people who die and are not saved. They go down quickly into hell through its wide opening. For those who say that hell does not exist, please do not deceive yourself just to ease your conscience. Hell is a real place. Hell even has gates with keys.

And I say also unto thee, That thou art Peter, and upon this rock I will build my church; and the gates of hell shall not prevail against it.

Matthew 16:18

I am he that liveth, and was dead; and, behold, I am alive for evermore, Amen; and have the keys of hell and of death.

Revelation 1:18

Hell has several gates which allow many to enter and these gates have several keys. The keeper of these keys is the master Jesus Himself. His heart is grieved each time disobedient mankind forces Him to unlock the gates. Remember, He does not wish to open these gates for you. He wants it to remain locked for the kingdom of darkness. Hell is the name of the entire place, however, the cells or chambers where people are imprisoned are called death. These chambers or cells can be likened to the prison cells on earth with inmates.

Her house is the way to hell, going down to the chambers of death.

Proverbs 7:27

These chambers are situated in a bottomless pit with sides.

As for thee also, by the blood of thy covenant I have sent forth thy prisoners out of the pit wherein is no water.

Zechariah 9:11

And the fifth angel sounded, and I saw a star fall from heaven unto the earth: and to him was given the key of the bottomless pit.

Revelation 9:1

Yet thou shalt be brought down to hell, to the sides of the pit.

Isaiah 14:15

I made the nations to shake at the sound of his fall, when I cast him down to hell with them that descend into the pit: and all the trees of Eden, the choice and best of Lebanon, all that drink water, shall be comforted in the nether parts of the earth.

Ezekiel 31:16

The entire pit is called *"the belly of hell"* as it has the ability to expand and enlarge itself.

And said, I cried by reason of mine affliction unto the Lord, and he heard me; out of the belly of hell cried I, and thou heardest my voice.

Jonah 2:2

Therefore hell hath enlarged herself, and opened her mouth without measure: and their glory, and their multitude, and their pomp, and he that rejoiceth, shall descend into it.

Isaiah 5:14

The word of God also describes hell as a place that is never full. This is because it automatically increases in size as more people are cast into it every second, minute and hour.

Hell and destruction are never full; so the eyes of man are never satisfied.

Proverbs 27:20

The word of God says that many there be which go to hell.

Enter ye in at the strait gate: for wide is the gate, and broad is the way, that leadeth to destruction, and many there be which go in thereat:

Matthew 7:13

❧❧

Chapter 6

30 REASONS WHY YOU SHOULD NOT GO TO HELL

Some people think that the world is hell because of the many atrocities in it. But the wickedness that is seen on the earth cannot be compared with that in hell. I have witnessed to people who have bluntly told me that they rather wish to go to hell. It is because they do not know what they are talking about. There are numerous reasons why you should not darken the doorstep of hell. Below are the reasons why you should not go to hell.

1. It is a place of sorrow.

The word sorrow is not a comfortable word for

anyone. No one wishes to intentionally experience sorrow for ever. On earth, people experience sorrow once a while when unfortunate things happen to them. But in hell, it is an everlasting sorrow. The sorrow has no end. The word of God says that hell is a place full of sorrow because everyone in hell is a sad person. There are no smiles in hell. No one laughs. They are all embedded in sorrow. You cannot receive encouragement from your neighbour because they all live in sorrow. I have experienced sorrow here on earth and I would not like to have such an experience forever.

The sorrows of hell compassed me about: the snares of death prevented me.

Psalm 18:5

2. It is a place of pain.

The pain that a mother experiences when giving birth cannot be compared with the pains of hell. The pain of those involved in traumatic accidents cannot be compared to the pains of hell. The pain that people experience when cut with a knife cannot be compared with the pains of hell. Hell is full of different and diverse forms of pain. Imagine living in pain forever. It is unimaginable. I have seen people in pain before and the expressions on their faces tells it all. One of the worst pains to have on earth is back pain but doctors can prescribe painkillers to subdue this pain. All the painkillers in the world put together cannot subdue the pains of hell. This is because it is forever.

The sorrows of death compassed me, and the pains of hell gat hold upon me: I found trouble and sorrow.

Psalm 116:3

3. It is a place full of troubles.

In hell, there is trouble in every direction you turn. This is because it is full of all the wicked and most troublesome people in this world, including the devil and his wicked workers. Think about any troublesome and wicked person in this world. Think about all the hardcore criminals who do not repent and then die in their sins. They will be your next door neighbour if you find yourself in hell. Hell itself is a place full of trouble with troublesome people.

The sorrows of death compassed me, and the pains of hell gat hold upon me: I found trouble and sorrow.

Psalm 116:3

4. It is a place of unquenchable fire.

The word of God encourages to do anything in order not to go to hell. This is because it is a place full of fire and the fire cannot be quenched with water. It cannot be quenched with any method that the fire service uses to quench fires. Those that go to hell are burnt in fire but they are not consumed by the fire. They will scream forever because the fire never stops burning. Your ears will be tormented by your own continuous screams and the shrieking of your inmates. There is such a commotion of noise due to the fire that is burning every prisoner of hell. The word of God emphatically states that the fire shall never be quenched.

And if thy foot offend thee, cut it off: it is better for thee to enter halt into life, than having two feet to be cast into hell, into the fire that never shall be quenched:

Where their worm dieth not, and the fire is not quenched.

Mark 9:45-46

But I say unto you, That whosoever is angry with his brother without a cause shall be in danger of the judgment: and whosoever shall say to his brother, Raca, shall be in danger of the council: but whosoever shall say, Thou fool, shall be in danger of hell fire.

Matthew 5:22

The fire in hell is an everlasting fire. It never goes out. It is always in flames.

Then shall he say also unto them on the left hand, Depart from me, ye cursed, into everlasting fire, prepared for the devil and his angels:

Matthew 25:41

5. It is a place full of worms.

The people that go to hell decay alive. They are alive but their bodies are being eaten away while they scream in pain. Because their bodies decay alive, they become full of worms. The worms do not die and they feed on their victims forever. Not even the fire that is burning them can kill these worms. Those of you that find a lot of things disgusting to you should never darken the door step of hell because it is a very smelly place. I can only imagine the sickening stench as these repulsive worms eat their victims alive.

Thy pomp is brought down to the grave, and the noise of thy viols: the worm is spread under thee, and the worms cover thee.

Isaiah 14:11

6. It is a place of continuous destruction.

A person is utterly destroyed once taken to hell. Hell itself is full of destruction. Satan enjoys causing pain to people and destroying them in whichever way he can. So if you find yourself in hell, you have done him a great favour to continue his destructive activities in your life forever.

And fear not them which kill the body, but are not able to kill the soul: but rather fear him which is able to destroy both soul and body in hell.

Matthew 10:28

Hell is naked before him, and destruction hath no covering.

Job 26:6

7. It is a place of eternal damnation and condemnation.

In the world, when a criminal is condemned for life, they can still live a very happy life while in prison.

They are well fed and are often given an ensuite room to sleep. I was once talking to someone in prison about what being in prison is like. This person said to me that he has everything including a television with many channels. The person said that the only thing someone in prison does not have is the freedom to live a real life like those who are not in prison. I have even noticed that some people who go to prison put on weight. At times, even the sentence of condemnation in the world can be overturned. It is not so in hell. All those who go to hell do not have the luxury of the prisons on the earth. They are condemned forever in a terrible prison. It is an eternal condemnation. It is forever without end.

And many of them that sleep in the dust of the earth shall awake, some to everlasting life, and some to shame and everlasting contempt.

Daniel 12:2

Ye serpents, ye generation of vipers, how can ye escape the damnation of hell?

Matthew 23:33

8. It is a place where you cannot die.

The pain, the sorrow and the destruction in hell is so intensive that you will wish and beg to die but you cannot. On earth, when people become fed up and think there is no hope, they sadly take their lives to end their frustrations. But it is not so in hell. You cannot take your own life. Being in hell means that you have no other choice than to endure everlasting pain.

Where their worm dieth not, and the fire is not quenched.

Mark 9:46

9. It is a home for demons who look like animals and fearsome creatures.

Avoid hell at all cost because your inmates and next door neighbours will be demons. These demons look like scary animals. They are very bizarre creatures that you would never want to meet in life let alone to live with them forever.

And I looked, and behold a pale horse: and his name that sat on him was Death, and Hell followed with him. And power was given unto them over the fourth part of the earth, to kill with sword, and with hunger, and with death, and with the beasts of the earth.

Revelation 6:8

And the fifth angel sounded, and I saw a star fall from heaven unto the earth: and to him was given the key of the bottomless pit.

And he opened the bottomless pit; and there arose a smoke out of the pit, as the smoke of a great furnace; and the sun and the air were darkened by reason of the smoke of the pit.

And there came out of the smoke locusts upon the earth: and unto them was given power, as the scorpions of the earth have power.

And it was commanded them that they should not hurt the grass of the earth, neither any green thing, neither any tree; but only those men which have not the seal of God in their foreheads.

And to them it was given that they should not kill them, but that they should be tormented five months: and their torment was as the torment of a scorpion, when he striketh a man.

And in those days shall men seek death, and shall not find it; and shall desire to die, and death shall flee from them.

And the shapes of the locusts were like unto horses prepared unto battle; and on their heads were as it were crowns like gold, and their faces were as the faces of men.

And they had hair as the hair of women, and their teeth were as the teeth of lions.

And they had breastplates, as it were breastplates of iron; and the sound of their wings was as the sound of chariots of many horses running to battle.

And they had tails like unto scorpions, and there were stings in their tails: and their power was to hurt men five months.

And they had a king over them, which is the angel of the bottomless pit, whose name in the Hebrew tongue is Abaddon, but in the Greek tongue hath his name Apollyon.

Revelation 9:1-11

And when they shall have finished their testimony, the beast that ascendeth out of the bottomless pit shall make war against them, and shall overcome them, and kill them.

Revelation 11:17

And he laid hold on the dragon, that old serpent, which is the Devil, and Satan, and bound him a thousand years,
Revelation 20:2

10. It is a place of total darkness.

When you are in your house and the lights go off, you struggle to find where things are because of the darkness. Yet the darkness in hell, which the Bible talks about, cannot be compared with the darkness in a house. It cannot even be compared to the darkness that occurs on earth when there is total eclipse of the moon. We are talking about darkness that is so thick that it can be touched. It is called darkness of darkness. Imagine being in this darkness for ever. I say of a truth, do whatever you can to escape hell for it is a place of total and utter darkness.

Thou hast laid me in the lowest pit, in darkness, in the deeps.
Psalm 88:6

11. It is a place of unending torments day and night.

Hell is a place of unending torture by Satan, demons and fallen angels. In the world, when a criminal is caught and they do not want to speak the truth, they are tortured painfully until they spill out the truth. I can tell you that no torture on earth can be compared to that in hell. Even on earth, the devil makes people blind, deaf, dumb, limbless and inflicts different kinds of sicknesses and diseases. This is how the devil torments people here on earth. He enjoy breaking marriages, making people addicted to drugs, making people commit murder, making people argue and fight and the list goes on. Imagine how the torture in hell will be like and it is forever. I would not like to be in such a place. The word of God states that the torture is day and night. Imagine being tortured day and night forever.

And the devil that deceived them was cast into the lake of fire and brimstone, where the beast and the false prophet are, and shall be tormented day and night for ever and ever.

Revelation 20:10

And in hell he lift up his eyes, being in torments, and seeth Abraham afar off, and Lazarus in his bosom.

And he cried and said, Father Abraham, have mercy on me, and send Lazarus, that he may dip the tip of his finger in water, and cool my tongue; for I am tormented in this flame.

Luke 16:23-24

12. It is a place of everlasting punishment.

It is a place where extremely severe punishment is inflicted upon those who end up there forever.

And these shall go away into everlasting punishment: but the righteous into life eternal.

Matthew 25:46

13. It is a place of everlasting contempt.

It is a place where you are hated day and night. There is nothing like friendliness and niceness in hell. This is because the demons of hell hate themselves as much as they hate humans. But in hell, all their hate is focused on those who find themselves there forever. Avoid hell at all cost. Advise your friends, relatives, work colleagues and others you meet on the street to avoid this place.

And many of them that sleep in the dust of the earth shall awake, some to everlasting life, and some to shame and everlasting contempt.

Daniel 12:2

14. Hell is full of smoke.

Hell is always on fire. This fire is never quenched

and therefore it generates smoke day and night. The word of God says that when hell, which is also known as the bottomless pit, was opened the smoke that rushed out was able to darken the air as well as the sun which is high above. What kind of smoke are we talking about? It is an everlasting smoke in the pit of hell. You do not want to be in such a place where you will be choked with smoke and inhaling poisonous smoke forever.

And he opened the bottomless pit; and there arose a smoke out of the pit, as the smoke of a great furnace; and the sun and the air were darkened by reason of the smoke of the pit.

Revelation 9:2

15. There is no water in hell.

Hell is a place of perpetual thirst. We waste so much water on earth. You can stay in the shower for hours. You can fill your bath to the brim and lie in it. You can buy 100 bottles of water and drink all of them. But it is not like that in hell. You cannot get a bottle of water or any form of water. It is a dry and thirsty place. The rich man begged Father Abraham in Luke 16, to tell Lazarus to dip the tip of his finger in a drop of water for him to drink.

He was begging for a drop of water in hell. This is serious. I drink a lot of water so I cannot imagine finding myself in a place where there is no water. Do not wish to be there.

And he cried and said, Father Abraham, have mercy on me, and send Lazarus, that he may dip the tip of his finger in water, and cool my tongue; for I am tormented in this flame.

Luke 16:24

As for thee also, by the blood of thy covenant I have sent forth thy prisoners out of the pit wherein is no water.

Zechariah 9:11

16. It is a place of weeping.

There is no joy in hell. It is therefore a place where weeping continues forever. This kind of torment is what those who go to hell experience. They can only weep and weep but it will be without remedy.

But the children of the kingdom shall be cast out into outer darkness: there shall be weeping and gnashing of teeth.

Matthew 8:12

17. It is a place of wailing.

This is a higher form of weeping. You will not just weep silently as the tears run down your cheeks, you will actually be screaming and wailing at the top of your voice without any help.

And shall cast them into a furnace of fire: there shall be wailing and gnashing of teeth.

Matthew 13:42

18. Hell is a furnace of fire.

When I was growing up back home in Ghana, I used to help my grandmother while she baked bread in a furnace of clay. We would put a lot of fire in the furnace and allow it to become very hot. The furnace becomes so hot that you have to first put the raw bread on a stick to push it in the furnace. This fire and its heat cannot be compared to that of hell because the whole of hell and hell itself is a furnace.

And shall cast them into the furnace of fire: there shall be wailing and gnashing of teeth.

Matthew 13:50

19. The king of hell is satan.

People are scared when they hear the name of satan or the devil mentioned. But their refusal to give their lives to Jesus will mean that they end up with the same devil they are running away from. The devil is the ruler, the prime minister and the president of hell. Do not meet him there, go to heaven instead.

And I saw an angel come down from heaven, having the key of the bottomless pit and a great chain in his hand.

And he laid hold on the dragon, that old serpent, which is the Devil, and Satan, and bound him a thousand years,

And cast him into the bottomless pit, and shut him up, and set a seal upon him, that he should deceive the nations no more, till the thousand years should be fulfilled: and after that he must be loosed a little season.

Revelation 20:1-3

And they had a king over them, which is the angel of the bottomless pit, whose name in the Hebrew tongue is Abaddon, but in the Greek tongue hath his name Apollyon.

Revelation 9:11

My brother, my sister, you have no reason to go to hell. All the work has been done for you and all you need to do is to accept what is yours. God with His unfailing love has prepared a better place for you called heaven. You must do everything necessary to avoid hell. Receive Jesus into your life. Love Him, serve Him and escape hell.

MORE REASONS WHY YOU SHOULD NOT GO TO HELL

20. Because God loves you.

God loves mankind so much that He did not want to see them perish in hell. He demonstrated His great love for us by sending His son Jesus Christ to rescue us.

For God so loved the world, that he gave his only begotten Son, that whosoever believeth in him should not perish, but have everlasting life.

John 3:16

21. God did not send Jesus to come and condemn you but to save you.

God knew that we were sinners and He still sent His son to come and die for us. He did not send Him to come and condemn us but to show us His love and to save us. Jesus did not come to judge us, He came to save us from our sins and to draw us closer to Himself.

For God sent not his Son into the world to condemn the world; but that the world through him might be saved.

John 3:17

But God commendeth his love toward us, in that, while we were yet sinners, Christ died for us.

Romans 5:8

22. God has paid the penalty of our sins through Jesus Christ. His life was the price for our sins.

God the Father sent His son Jesus to die for the sins of mankind. We owed a debt to the devil and nothing could pay for it except a life. This life was the only price that could settle our debt. The life was the life of God's dear son Jesus Christ.

The word "ransom" below in 1 Timothy 2:4-6 means *"a price."* This price has been paid for you and me so that we should not go to hell.

Who will have all men to be saved, and to come unto the knowledge of the truth.

For there is one God, and one mediator between God and men, the man Christ Jesus;

Who gave himself a ransom for all, to be testified in due time.

1 Timothy 2:4-6

23. Jesus became our sins on the cross.

Jesus did not just die for our sins, He actually became our sins. The word of God states that God made Him to be sin that we might become God's righteousness.

For he hath made him to be sin for us, who knew no sin; that we might be made the righteousness of God in him.

2 Corinthians 5:21

24. Jesus became our substitute when He died on the cross.

Jesus became the replacement for our sins. Remember that He never sinned. Yet because of our sins He became sin, so that when God looks at us He cannot see our sins. All that He sees is the blood of Jesus Christ that was shed for our sins on the cross.

And he is the propitiation for our sins: and not for ours only, but also for the sins of the whole world.

1 John 2:2

Herein is love, not that we loved God, but that he loved us, and sent his Son to be the propitiation for our sins.

1 John 4:10

Whom God hath set forth to be a propitiation through faith in his blood, to declare his righteousness for the remission of sins that are past, through the forbearance of God;

Romans 3:25

Jesus bought us with His life from Satan when He died on the cross. Jesus paid the price for our sins with His life so satan does not have the right to take us to hell. When you purchase something from a shop and you pay for it, the shop owner does not come to your house the following day to collect the item you have bought. Do not allow the devil to deceive you. The blood of Jesus has paid for our past sins, present sins and our future sins if we confess them. You do not owe the devil a penny. Tell him to get out of your life in Jesus name.

For ye are bought with a price: therefore glorify God in your body, and in your spirit, which are God's.

1 Corinthians 6:20

25. Jesus was nailed to the cross and died a shameful death because of our sins.

Jesus had to die a shameful and painful death on the cross as a replacement for wicked and sinful mankind. You see, crucifixion was a form of severe capital punishment practised by many nations in the past, especially by the Romans. It was the highest form of capital punishment. The crimes committed by those killed this way were considered heinous and it was performed publicly to shame, terrorise and warn others from committing the same crimes. Those convicted were executed in this way so as to die slowly and painfully. Some were crucified on the cross while others were placed on stakes with the sticks passing through their groin.

It was gruesome and caused excruciating pain. Those crucified this way were then allowed to die slowly and painfully as each muscle, fibre and nerve is stretched to its limits of agony. For Christ, nails were pierced through His arms and feet with the body bearing its full weight on the feet and arms. What kind of cruelty is this? This is to highlight to you the kind of pain that Jesus went through to secure victory for mankind on the cross. Jesus never sinned while on the earth and He did not deserve to die on the cross. He committed no crimes and yet, He was crucified on the cross to pay the penalty for our sins.

For we have not an high priest which cannot be touched with the feeling of our infirmities; but was in all points tempted like as we are, yet without sin.

Hebrews 4:15

For he hath made him to be sin for us, who knew no sin; that we might be made the righteousness of God in him.

2 Corinthians 5:21

Even though Jesus committed no crimes while on the earth, He was treated by His killers as a sinner. He suffered and died on the cross for us. He nailed all our weaknesses, shame, curses, sicknesses, diseases and all that the devil had against us on the cross.

Blotting out the handwriting of ordinances that was against us, which was contrary to us, and took it out of the way, nailing it to his cross;

Colossians 2:14

The Son of God was mocked and killed because of our sins. They stripped Him naked and shared His clothes among themselves. He did not deserve to die in such a shameful way and yet He chose to die in our place. We were supposed to be on that cross. Those big nails were supposed to pierce through our hands and feet but Jesus chose to go through that pain for the sake of mankind. Do not go to hell because He has done this for you.

And they crucified him, and parted his garments, casting lots: that it might be fulfilled which was spoken by the prophet, They parted my garments among them, and upon my vesture did they cast lots.

Matthew 27:35

26. All our sins and the guilt of sins are washed away by the blood of Jesus.

You no longer have to live life with the guilt of your sins. When God forgives, He takes away the guilt too. The blood of Jesus washes us and makes us as white as snow.

How much more shall the blood of Christ, who through the eternal Spirit offered himself without spot to God, purge your conscience from dead works to serve the living God?

Hebrews 9:14

And from Jesus Christ, who is the faithful witness, and the first begotten of the dead, and the prince of the kings of the earth. Unto him that loved us, and washed us from our sins in his own blood,

Revelation 1:5

27. You do not have to go to hell because God can give you a brand new life in Jesus Christ.

When you give your life to Jesus, you become a new person. Your old life is stripped off you by the blood of Jesus.

Therefore if any man be in Christ, he is a new creature: old things are passed away; behold, all things are become new.

2 Corinthians 5:17

28. All the work has been done for you and you only have to accept God's love.

Other religions tell you to do this and do that but with God the Creator of heaven and earth, He says all is done. It is finished.

When Jesus therefore had received the vinegar, he said, It is finished: and he bowed his head, and gave up the ghost.

John 19:30

29. Hell was not made for you and you should avoid it at all cost.

God has promised to receive all that come to Him. He said He will never send you away when you come to Him.

All that the Father giveth me shall come to me; and him that cometh to me I will in no wise cast out.

John 6:7

God does not want anyone to perish in his or her sins.

The Lord is not slack concerning his promise, as some men count slackness; but is longsuffering to us-ward, not willing that any should perish, but that all should come to repentance.

2 Peter 3:9

God wants everyone to be saved.

Who will have all men to be saved, and to come unto

the knowledge of the truth.

1 Timothy 2:4

The grace of God that brings salvation has been made available to all men.

For the grace of God that bringeth salvation hath appeared to all men.

Titus 2:11

30. **Finally, hell was made for Satan, his fallen angels and all who are disobedient to the Lord and live all their lives for Satan.**

Hell was not made for mankind. It was made for Satan and all his fallen angels. All those who do not accept Jesus Christ as their Lord and continue to live in sin and worship Satan will go to hell if they die in their sins. I will emphasise again that hell was not made for you and you should not go there by choice. The passage of scripture below tells us that hell has been prepared for the devil and his angels.

Then shall he say also unto them on the left hand, Depart from me, ye cursed, into everlasting fire, prepared for the devil and his angels:

Matthew 25:41

*Father, give us the nations for our
inheritance and the ends of the earth
for our possession.
Send me to the nations to propagate
the gospel of Jesus Christ.
Raise me up and give me the fire to go.
Father, may I not live unto myself but
live to see others saved.
I am ready oh Lord for Your use and
I am ready to sacrifice my life to see
others saved.
Send me on the missions oh Lord.
Lead me Lord and I will follow, lead
me and I will go. Amen*

༺≈༻

Chapter 7

GO!!!!!!!!!!!!!!!!!!!!!!!!

I can literally see Jesus screaming with a loud voice, telling the disciples to GO!!!!!!!!!!!! I can imagine the disciples being lazy and unwilling to do anything to bring souls into the kingdom. I can see the Christians in Jesus' day being so comfortable in their Christianity that they do not witness to anyone to receive the kingdom of God. I can see the churches in those days only using the power of God as a source of receiving material things and not using it for winning souls for the Lord. I can see the churches not organising evangelism to bring souls into the kingdom. I can see the churches not sending missionaries to the furthest parts of the world. This is what Jesus saw happening to the disciples, to Christians, to churches and to pastors in those days. Jesus could see the pastors not working hard to bring souls into His kingdom. So He literally yelled at them to GO!!!!!!!!!!!!

And he said unto them, Go ye into all the world, and preach the gospel to every creature.

He that believeth and is baptized shall be saved; but he that believeth not shall be damned.

Mark 16:15-16

Go ye therefore, and teach all nations, baptizing them in the name of the Father, and of the Son, and of the Holy Ghost:

Teaching them to observe all things whatsoever I have commanded you: and, lo, I am with you alway, even unto the end of the world. Amen.

Matthew 28:19-20

The same evil is happening to Christians and churches today. Christians do not think about heaven even to witness to someone about Jesus. No one seems to care about the souls that are perishing every second, every minute, every hour and every day. Churches are no longer winning souls for the kingdom of God. They are not sending out missionaries to countries to win souls for Christ. Churches have become so lazy to go into the world and preach the gospel. Pastors have shifted from the main reason why they are pastors in the first place and that is to win the lost at all cost. Jesus told the Pharisees that they had forgotten the weightier matters of God's law.

Woe unto you, scribes and Pharisees, hypocrites! for ye pay tithe of mint and anise and cummin, and have omitted the weightier matters of the law, judgment, mercy, and faith: these ought ye to have done, and not to leave the other undone.

Matthew 23:23

Pastors have certainly forgotten the weightier matters of the law. They have forgotten their job description. We have become concerned with driving nice cars, living in nice houses, organising programs that bring more money to our churches, organising programs that do not yield souls and writing books that do not bring people closer to the Lord. When you listen to the messages some pastors preach, you wonder whether they are preaching from the Bible. This is the reason why Christians have become money seekers and "bless me" Christians.

When I became a Christian, all the messages

I heard my pastor preached were centered on soul winning and bringing the lost to Christ. Therefore, as a baby Christian, I began to do person to person evangelism. I did not even know much of the scriptures but I wanted to witness to others. I remember the first message I preached when I went for evangelism. I said, "if you do not have Jesus, you are like a paper being blown by the wind and it can blow you in any direction." When I remember my first message I laugh, but I was determined to win the lost because of the messages my pastor preached. I have continued in that same vein and today I am a pastor and I am also encouraging my church members to win the lost for Christ. If we are going to win the world for Christ, we must change our attitude towards soul winning and heed to the word "GO", a commandment from our master Jesus Christ. We all have to roll our sleeves back and get to work, the work of winning souls for Jesus.

Who Should Go

The burden of who should go is on the body of Christ. It is the greatest commission that Jesus commanded the body of Christ to accomplish whilst on the earth. Jesus said GO with you in mind. Jesus said GO with all Christians in mind. Jesus said GO with all Apostles, Prophets, Evangelists, Pastors and Teachers in mind. Jesus said GO with all the churches worldwide in mind. Jesus said GO with the body of Christ in mind. Therefore, the word GO does not leave room for any member of the body of Christ to sit on the fence.

But unfortunately, we have left this great work of wining souls for a select few in the body of Christ. Jesus was not only speaking to the evangelist. Yes, the evangelist has a special anointing to bring souls to Jesus but each and every one who is a member of the body of Christ is also mandated to preach the gospel. I must stress the fact that no matter what kind of calling you have; be it Apostle, Prophet, Evangelist, Pastor or Teacher, your first duty is to bring the lost to Christ. Some so called prophets of these days only know how to prophesy money and blessings to the people of God. I want to say to all such prophets, you also have a duty to win the lost for Jesus.

Ordinary Christians can be trained to witness for the Lord and congregations can be trained to win souls for Jesus. In fact, anyone who professes to be a follower of Christ can win souls for the Lord. God wants to save the whole world and He employs every believer or Christian to heed His call to go and preach the gospel. Jesus said that the harvest is great but the labourers are few. Jesus is crying for more labourers, more believers, more Christians and more preachers to heed the call to go and win the lost.

Therefore said he unto them, The harvest truly is great, but the labourers are few: pray ye therefore the Lord of the harvest, that he would send forth labourers into his harvest.

Luke 10:2

One day I had a dream in which I saw Father Abraham. In the dream, I saw a tall handsome man. I immediately knew in my heart that it was Father Abraham. In the dream, Father Abraham asked me to follow him. He led me into a rocky ground which was being used as a shelter for people preparing for the end time work of the Lord. Some of the people were praying, others were rehearsing and preparing. They had only one aim and the aim was to do the work of the Lord. Father Abraham called all the people to gather and he asked me to stand in the middle for them to pray for me.

As soon as the prayers finished, my eyes opened. I realised the Lord had called me to His end time work of winning souls for the kingdom of God. I have been trained and equipped to go and preach the gospel and ordinary Christians can be equipped to do God's work and preach the gospel.

Where to Go

The word "GO" comes from the Greek word "Poreuomai" which means *"to travel, to depart, to go away, go forth, to take a journey and to walk."* It does not in any way suggest standing still or sitting at one place. It shows movement by Christians, ordinary believers, churches, apostles, prophets, evangelists, pastors and teachers to go and preach the gospel to the lost souls. Jesus was very specific as to where Christians are supposed to go and preach the gospel. Our destination is the whole world, our vision is the whole world and our job description is to win the entire world for Christ.

Go ye into all the world and preach the gospel to every creature...

Mark 16:15

We are to witness to the nations of the world. We do not have to just stay in our own countries, we must go to every country in the world.

Go ye therefore, and teach all nations....

Matthew 28:19

We are to go and preach to everyone. We must not be selective of who to preach to. God has sent us to preach to every kindred, every tongue, every people and every nation. Preach to the white, black, red, gold, green and blue human beings. Jesus has shed His blood for all mankind.

And they sung a new song, saying, Thou art worthy to take the book, and to open the seals thereof: for thou wast slain, and hast redeemed us to God by thy blood out of every kindred, and tongue, and people, and nation;

Revelation 5:9

The word of God states that when the Holy Spirit comes upon us, we will become witnesses in Jerusalem, Judaea, Samaria and the uttermost part of the earth.

But ye shall receive power, after that the Holy Ghost is come upon you: and ye shall be witnesses unto me both in Jerusalem, and in all Judaea, and in Samaria, and unto the uttermost part of the earth.

Acts 1:8

Our Jerusalem is where we are. This means that we must first witness to those in our everyday surroundings. You can start with your family members, your friends, your neighbours, your work colleagues and then to the streets and then to the nations. Judaea is moving from where you are and going a bit further into the surrounding areas. Samaria is preaching within the entire country where you live and the uttermost part of the world means going to every nation and every country in the world. I strongly believe that this is how all churches are supposed to operate. We must first start a church in the village and city where we are, which is our Jerusalem. We must then start branches in the village or city where we are, which is our Judaea. We must then spread and start branches in the whole of the country where we planted the first church. This will be our Samaria. Most countries have several cities and villages and churches must be started in all of them. The end of the call is to ensure that you have planted churches in every country and nation of the world through missionaries.

We must train and send missionaries to preach and start churches in every nation. This will be the uttermost part of the earth. This process of reaching the world restarts as the missionary goes to a country and plants a church. Remember that the uttermost part of the earth is very important because the gospel must first be published in every country on the earth before the end of the world will come.

And the gospel must first be published among all nations.
Mark 13:10

Any pastor whose vision is to have a large congregation at one place without training his church members to be able to start churches, to witness and evangelise the world, does not have the vision of Jesus Christ to save the whole world. Any church that does not send out missionaries is a selfish church. That church is not heeding the call to go into all the world to preach the gospel. We should not be too comfortable where we are. One of the meanings of the word GO is *"to travel."* We must send missionaries to travel to other countries. People must depart to the other parts of the world to fulfil the Great Commission.

❧

Chapter 8

PREPARATION TO GO

The most common problem among believers is that they do not know what to say when they meet someone who is not saved. This is usually due to a lack of confidence, lack of knowledge of the scriptures or because the believer is still living in sin. Firstly, Christians must be taught how to live a holy life. This will give them the confidence to witness to others without fear. The word of God states that the righteous are as bold as a lion.

The wicked flee when no man pursueth: but the righteous are bold as a lion.

Proverbs 28:1

When a person lives in sin, they have no boldness to witness. Sin greatly hinders their ability to function as a labourer for the Lord. Christians who still enjoy the pleasure of sin cannot be good witnesses for the Lord. Pastors must therefore teach holiness in their churches.

But in a great house there are not only vessels of gold and of silver, but also of wood and of earth; and some to honour, and some to dishonour.

If a man therefore purge himself from these, he shall be a vessel unto honour, sanctified, and meet for the master's use, and prepared unto every good work.

2 Timothy 2:20-21

Secondly, Christians must prepare by reading the Bible, studying it and memorising key evangelistic scriptures. Knowing the scriptures will equip the Christian to answer questions that the lost souls tend to ask during witnessing. The word of God entreats us to know how to answer every man.

Let your speech be alway with grace, seasoned with salt, that ye may know how ye ought to answer every man.

Colossians 4:6

Thirdly, we must pray in preparation to witness. No Christian can convert a soul, it is the work of the Holy Spirit.

Nevertheless I tell you the truth; It is expedient for you that I go away: for if I go not away, the Comforter will not come unto you; but if I depart, I will send him unto you.

John 16:7

We must therefore pray to the Lord to win the souls as we witness. We are just vessels for Him to work through. Spend time with God and ask the Holy Spirit to witness through you to the people you are going to preach to. Ask the Holy Spirit to back your words with the power of God. The Holy Spirit is the Spirit that testifies Jesus to others. He will speak through us.

But when the Comforter is come, whom I will send unto you from the Father, even the Spirit of truth, which proceedeth from the Father, he shall testify of me:

John 15:26

The Lord of the harvest knows how to win the souls. We must pray to God to allow the Holy Spirit to lead us. He is the Lord of the harvest.

Pray ye therefore the Lord of the harvest, that he will send forth labourers into his harvest.

Matthew 9:38

Lastly, in order for evangelism to be effective, we must constantly pray for the Holy Spirit to come upon us. The word of God states that, when He the Holy Spirit comes upon us, we will receive power to be witnesses. We must therefore constantly pray for the Holy Spirit to come upon us in order to be effective witnesses.

But ye shall receive power, after that the Holy Ghost is come upon you: and ye shall be witnesses unto me both in Jerusalem, and in all Judaea, and in Samaria, and unto the uttermost part of the earth.

Acts 1:8

KEY SCRIPTURES FOR EVANGELISM

For all have sinned, and come short of the glory of God;

Romans 3:23

For the wages of sin is death; but the gift of God is eternal life through Jesus Christ our Lord.

Romans 6:23

And as it is appointed unto men once to die, but after this the judgment:

Hebrews 9:27

But God commendeth his love toward us, in that, while we were yet sinners, Christ died for us.

Romans 5:8

For God so loved the world, that he gave his only begotten Son, that whosoever believeth in him should not perish, but have everlasting life.

John 3:16

For God sent not his Son into the world to condemn the world; but that the world through him might be saved.

John 3:17

For God shall bring every work into judgment, with every secret thing, whether it be good, or whether it be evil.

Ecclesiastes 12:14

Neither is there salvation in any other: for there is none other name under heaven given among men, whereby we must be saved.

Acts 4:12

That if thou shalt confess with thy mouth the Lord Jesus, and shalt believe in thine heart that God hath raised him from the dead, thou shalt be saved.

Romans 10:9

For with the heart man believeth unto righteousness; and with the mouth confession is made unto salvation.

Romans 10:10

For we must all appear before the judgment seat of Christ; that every one may receive the things done in his body, according to that he hath done, whether it be good or bad.

2 Corinthians 5:10

But we are all as an unclean thing, and all our righteousnesses are as filthy rags; and we all do fade as a leaf; and our iniquities, like the wind, have taken us away.

Isaiah 64:6

For what is a man profited, if he shall gain the whole world, and lose his own soul? or what shall a man give in exchange for his soul?

Matthew 16:26

Enter ye in at the strait gate: for wide is the gate, and broad is the way, that leadeth to destruction, and many there be which go in thereat:

Matthew 7:13

Because strait is the gate, and narrow is the way, which leadeth unto life, and few there be that find it.

Matthew 7:14

But as many as received him, to them gave he power to become the sons of God, even to them that believe on his name:

John 1:12

Jesus saith unto him, I am the way, the truth, and the life: no man cometh unto the Father, but by me.

John 14:6

Knowing this first, that there shall come in the last days scoffers, walking after their own lusts,

And saying, Where is the promise of his coming? for since the fathers fell asleep, all things continue as they were from the beginning of the creation.

For this they willingly are ignorant of, that by the word of God the heavens were of old, and the earth standing out of the water and in the water:

Whereby the world that then was, being overflowed with water, perished:

But the heavens and the earth, which are now, by the same word are kept in store, reserved unto fire against the day of judgment and perdition of ungodly men.

But, beloved, be not ignorant of this one thing, that one day is with the Lord as a thousand years, and a thousand years as one day.

The Lord is not slack concerning his promise, as some men count slackness; but is longsuffering to us-ward, not willing that any should perish, but that all should come to repentance.

But the day of the Lord will come as a thief in the night; in the which the heavens shall pass away with a great noise, and the elements shall melt with fervent heat, the earth also and the works that are therein shall be burned up.

2 Peter 3:3-10

Who will have all men to be saved, and to come unto the knowledge of the truth.

For there is one God, and one mediator between God and men, the man Christ Jesus;

Who gave himself a ransom for all, to be testified in due time.

1 Timothy 2:4-6

For by grace are ye saved through faith; and that not of yourselves: it is the gift of God: Not of works, lest any man should boast.

Ephesians 2:8-9

Therefore if any man be in Christ, he is a new creature: old things are passed away; behold, all things are become new.

2 Corinthians 5:17

There was a man of the Pharisees, named Nicodemus, a ruler of the Jews:

The same came to Jesus by night, and said unto him, Rabbi, we know that thou art a teacher come from God: for no man can do these miracles that thou doest, except God be with him.

Jesus answered and said unto him, Verily, verily, I say unto thee, Except a man be born again, he cannot see the kingdom of God.

Nicodemus saith unto him, How can a man be born when he is old? can he enter the second time into his mother's womb, and be born?

Jesus answered, Verily, verily, I say unto thee, Except a man be born of water and of the Spirit, he cannot enter into the kingdom of God.

That which is born of the flesh is flesh; and that which is born of the Spirit is spirit.

Marvel not that I said unto thee, Ye must be born again.
John 3:1-7

Put them in mind to be subject to principalities and powers, to obey magistrates, to be ready to every good work,

To speak evil of no man, to be no brawlers, but gentle, shewing all meekness unto all men.

For we ourselves also were sometimes foolish, disobedient, deceived, serving divers lusts and pleasures, living in malice and envy, hateful, and hating one another.

But after that the kindness and love of God our Saviour toward man appeared,

Not by works of righteousness which we have done, but according to his mercy he saved us, by the washing of regeneration, and renewing of the Holy Ghost;

Titus 3:1-5

The fool hath said in his heart, There is no God. Corrupt are they, and have done abominable iniquity: there is none that doeth good.

Psalm 53:1

WHAT TO DO AND WHAT NOT TO DO WHEN YOU GO

1. Preach the gospel of the cross to the person.

When you approach an individual who needs salvation, tell the person about Jesus Christ. Preach to the person that Jesus came to die for our sins. Tell the person that Jesus was crucified on the cross for our sins, He was buried and He rose again on the third day. This is the whole gospel of Jesus Christ. He was sent to the earth by God the Father, He was crucified on the cross, He was buried and He rose again from the dead on the third day.

Moreover, brethren, I declare unto you the gospel which I preached unto you, which also ye have received, and wherein ye stand;

By which also ye are saved, if ye keep in memory what I preached unto you, unless ye have believed in vain.

For I delivered unto you first of all that which I also received, how that Christ died for our sins according to the scriptures;

And that he was buried, and that he rose again the third day according to the scriptures:

And that he was seen of Cephas, then of the twelve:

After that, he was seen of above five hundred brethren at once; of whom the greater part remain unto this present, but some are fallen asleep.

After that, he was seen of James; then of all the apostles.
1 Corinthians 15:1-7

It is the preaching of the cross that has the power to save the lost. Our human wisdom is not good enough to save a soul but the preaching of the cross has mighty power to save.

For the preaching of the cross is to them that perish foolishness; but unto us which are saved it is the power of God.

1 Corinthians 1:18

2. Tell them how and why you got saved.

Do not hide your past from the person. Tell the person what you were doing before you surrendered to Jesus Christ. This has the power to lead the individual concerned to Christ. The individual will realise that they are not the only sinner on earth for all have sinned and fallen short of the glory of God.

For all have sinned, and come short of the glory of God;
Romans 3:23

Every Christian was saved from the kingdom of darkness, which is Satan's kingdom, into the kingdom of light which is God's kingdom. Sometimes we Christians behave as if we are holy angels without any past. When we approach the unsaved, we often make them feel as if we have never sinned before and therefore they become defensive while we are witnessing to them. Let them know that you were once a sinner condemned but now you are saved and washed by the blood of Jesus.

Giving thanks unto the Father, which hath made us meet to be partakers of the inheritance of the saints in light:

Who hath delivered us from the power of darkness, and hath translated us into the kingdom of his dear Son:

In whom we have redemption through his blood, even the forgiveness of sins:

Colossians 1:12-14

Tell the person that you were once a drug addict but Jesus saved you. Tell them you were once a prostitute but Jesus saved you. Tell them you were once a liar and a thief but Jesus saved you. Tell the person that you used to sleep around but Jesus saved you. Tell them that you were once a drunkard but Jesus delivered you. Let the person know that you were in the world before and Jesus saved you. Tell them that if you are saved then he or she can also be saved. This is your testimony, that Jesus pulled you out from your mess and cleaned you up. Do not present yourself as a holier than thou kind of person to the individual you are witnessing to. If you do that, the first thing the unsaved soul will say is "do not judge me." As soon as that happens, the individual will not open their heart to receive the gospel.

For we ourselves also were sometimes foolish, disobedient, deceived, serving divers lusts and pleasures, living in malice and envy, hateful, and hating one another.

But after that the kindness and love of God our Saviour toward man appeared,

Not by works of righteousness which we have done, but according to his mercy he saved us, by the washing of regeneration, and renewing of the Holy Ghost;

Which he shed on us abundantly through Jesus Christ our Saviour;

Titus 3:3-6

Apostle Paul constantly told the people he was witnessing to what happened before he was converted and accepted Jesus Christ as his Lord and Saviour. He told King Agrippa of how he persecuted and killed the Christians and put them in prison. Read the passage of scripture below.

Then Agrippa said unto Paul, Thou art permitted to speak for thyself. Then Paul stretched forth the hand, and answered for himself:

I think myself happy, king Agrippa, because I shall answer for myself this day before thee touching all the things whereof I am accused of the Jews:

Especially because I know thee to be expert in all customs and questions which are among the Jews: wherefore I beseech thee to hear me patiently.

My manner of life from my youth, which was at the first among mine own nation at Jerusalem, know all the Jews;

Which knew me from the beginning, if they would testify, that after the most straitest sect of our religion I lived a Pharisee.

And now I stand and am judged for the hope of the promise made of God unto our fathers:

Unto which promise our twelve tribes, instantly serving God day and night, hope to come. For which hope's sake, king Agrippa, I am accused of the Jews.

Why should it be thought a thing incredible with you, that God should raise the dead?

I verily thought with myself, that I ought to do many things contrary to the name of Jesus of Nazareth.

Which thing I also did in Jerusalem: and many of the saints did I shut up in prison, having received authority from the chief priests; and when they were put to death, I gave my voice against them.

And I punished them oft in every synagogue, and compelled them to blaspheme; and being exceedingly mad against them, I persecuted them even unto strange cities.

Whereupon as I went to Damascus with authority and commission from the chief priests,

At midday, O king, I saw in the way a light from heaven, above the brightness of the sun, shining round about me and them which journeyed with me.

And when we were all fallen to the earth, I heard a voice speaking unto me, and saying in the Hebrew tongue, Saul, Saul, why persecutest thou me? it is hard for thee to kick against the pricks.

And I said, Who art thou, Lord? And he said, I am Jesus whom thou persecutest.

But rise, and stand upon thy feet: for I have appeared unto thee for this purpose, to make thee a minister and a witness both of these things which thou hast seen, and of those things in the which I will appear unto thee;

Delivering thee from the people, and from the Gentiles, unto whom now I send thee,

To open their eyes, and to turn them from darkness to light, and from the power of Satan unto God, that they may receive forgiveness of sins, and inheritance among them which are sanctified by faith that is in me.

Whereupon, O king Agrippa, I was not disobedient unto the heavenly vision:

Acts 26:1-19

3. Tell them why they need salvation.

I have met people who tell me they are good people and therefore they do not need salvation. You have to convince them, by the help of the Holy Spirit, that they need salvation. The word of God says in Romans 3:23 that all of us have sinned. It also states in Ecclesiastes 7:20 that there is no man in the whole earth who does good and does not sin. We all have a sinful nature and we sin every day.

David even confessed in Psalm 51:5 that *"in sin did my mother conceive me."* The word of God emphasises in Romans 3:10 that there is no single person in this world who is righteous. If you read all the above scriptures carefully, you can only conclude that no one is good enough for heaven except if he or she comes to Jesus. Read the following scriptures.

For all have sinned, and come short of the glory of God;
Romans 3:23

For there is not a just man upon earth, that doeth good, and sinneth not.
Ecclesiastes 7:20

As it is written, There is none righteous, no, not one:
Romans 3:10

Behold, I was shapen in iniquity; and in sin did my mother conceive me.
Psalm 51:5

This is why we all need salvation because we cannot save ourselves. How can an armed robber change to be a good person in society? How can a murderer convert and become a good person in society? You see, a sinful person cannot resolve to stop sinning unless the power of sin is broken by receiving Jesus Christ as their Lord and Saviour. The power of sin is broken as soon as you are saved.

For sin shall not have dominion over you: for ye are not under the law, but under grace.

Romans 6:14

4. Tell them that Jesus wants to take their burdens away.

Salvation is to our advantage. We have nothing to give to God but He has so many things to give to us. We come to Him with all our sins, our problems, curses and various burdens and we receive eternal life and all His goodness and His blessings. God wants to give us rest from our problems. Jesus said, *"Come unto me, all ye that labour and are heavy laden, and I will give you rest."* Tell the individual concerned to surrender to Jesus so that their burdens will be taken away.

Come unto me, all ye that labour and are heavy laden, and I will give you rest.

Take my yoke upon you, and learn of me; for I am meek and lowly in heart: and ye shall find rest unto your souls.

For my yoke is easy, and my burden is light.

Matthew 11:28-30

5. Do not argue with them.

This is a very important part of the witnessing process. No matter what happens, you must by all means try and avoid arguments. A lot of unsaved souls have at least one or two scriptures that they use to be defensive and argue their way out. If you ask questions that generate arguments, you enter into a zone where you cannot win.

But avoid foolish questions, and genealogies, and contentions, and strivings about the law; for they are unprofitable and vain.

Titus 3:9

6. Do not judge them.

Remember that you are a not a judge, you are a witness. You are not there to tell the person that he or she is a sinner. This will put the person off and generate a closed heart and mind. The person will switch off and whatever else you say will not work. Your aim is for the Holy Spirit to convict the person of their sins so that they will accept Jesus Christ. Do not take the position of the Holy Spirit. He knows how to do His job better than you the witness. Just preach the gospel and the Holy Spirit will do the rest. Never be in the position of a judge.

Two men went up into the temple to pray; the one a Pharisee, and the other a publican.

The Pharisee stood and prayed thus with himself, God, I thank thee, that I am not as other men are, extortioners, unjust, adulterers, or even as this publican.

Luke 18:10-11

7. Use wisdom when winning souls.

The word of God states that he that wins souls is a wise person. This means that we must be wise in winning the lost. You need wisdom to answer the questions that the unsaved are likely to ask. You need the wisdom of the scriptures. You need the wisdom of the Holy Spirit in order to win the lost. Pray to God for wisdom in winning the lost.

The fruit of the righteous is a tree of life; and he that winneth souls is wise.

Proverbs 11:30

8. Lead them to say the prayer of salvation.

After you have witnessed to the person and he or she decides to accept Jesus Christ as their Lord and Saviour, you can lead them to say the prayer of salvation. Let them know that they have to confess with their mouth Jesus Christ as their Lord and Saviour and believe in their heart that God has raised Him from the dead.

That if thou shalt confess with thy mouth the Lord Jesus, and shalt believe in thine heart that God hath raised him from the dead, thou shalt be saved.

For with the heart man believeth unto righteousness; and with the mouth confession is made unto salvation.
Romans 10:9-10

An Example of the Prayer of Salvation

My Father in heaven, I recognise that I am a sinner. I recognise that the Lord Jesus died for me and paid the penalty of my sins. Dear Lord, today I repent of my sins and I accept

Jesus Christ as my Lord and my Saviour.
Wash me with your blood and make me holy.
Please write my name in the book of life and give me
the grace to serve you for the rest of my life.
Thank you that I am born again.
Amen.

LIKELY QUESTIONS THE UNSAVED MAY ASK AND HOW TO ANSWER THEM

1. **I am a good person, I am not a sinner and therefore I do not need salvation.**

In the first place, the word of God says that there is not one good person on the earth who does not sin. You may do good for three weeks and then sin for one year. That is why the word of God says that there is no righteous person on the earth, not even one. The word of God also says that all our righteousness or good things we do are like filthy rags. This means that we can do a lot of good in our lives and still go to hell. Our good deeds cannot save us unless we accept Jesus Christ as our Lord and personal Saviour.

For there is not a just man upon earth, that doeth good, and sinneth not.

Ecclesiastes 7:20

As it is written, There is none righteous, no, not one:
                                        Romans 3:10

But we are all as an unclean thing, and all our righteousnesses are as filthy rags; and we all do fade as a leaf; and our iniquities, like the wind, have taken us away.
                                        Isaiah 64:6

2. **If God is God and He is all powerful, why does He not save everyone when He knows we are going to hell?**

In the beginning, sin was not in the world. God created everything perfect in Genesis chapter one. God said that all that He had created was good. God gave Adam a choice to choose to obey Him or not. But when the devil deceived Adam and Eve in the Garden of Eden, sin entered into the world. Because Adam chose to obey the devil, sin came into the world.

Now the serpent was more subtil than any beast of the field which the LORD God had made. And he said unto the woman, Yea, hath God said, Ye shall not eat of every tree of the garden?

And the woman said unto the serpent, We may eat of the fruit of the trees of the garden:

But of the fruit of the tree which is in the midst of the garden, God hath said, Ye shall not eat of it, neither shall ye touch it, lest ye die.

And the serpent said unto the woman, Ye shall not surely die:

For God doth know that in the day ye eat thereof, then your eyes shall be opened, and ye shall be as gods, knowing good and evil.

And when the woman saw that the tree was good for food, and that it was pleasant to the eyes, and a tree to be desired to make one wise, she took of the fruit thereof, and did eat, and gave also unto her husband with her; and he did eat.

And the eyes of them both were opened, and they knew that they were naked; and they sewed fig leaves together, and made themselves aprons.

And they heard the voice of the LORD God walking in the garden in the cool of the day: and Adam and his wife hid themselves from the presence of the LORD God amongst the trees of the garden.

And the LORD God called unto Adam, and said unto him, Where art thou?

And he said, I heard thy voice in the garden, and I was afraid, because I was naked; and I hid myself.

And he said, Who told thee that thou wast naked? Hast thou eaten of the tree, whereof I commanded thee that thou shouldest not eat?

And the man said, The woman whom thou gavest to be with me, she gave me of the tree, and I did eat.

And the LORD God said unto the woman, What is this that thou hast done? And the woman said, The serpent beguiled me, and I did eat.

And the LORD God said unto the serpent, Because thou hast done this, thou art cursed above all cattle, and above every beast of the field; upon thy belly shalt thou go, and dust shalt thou eat all the days of thy life:
Genesis 3:1-14

Now, just as God gave Adam a choice, every human being also has a choice to serve God or not. God is a just God and He will not force Himself on you. He will not force you to serve Him, you have to choose to do so.

Think about it. Before you go to the hospital, your local GP must refer you. But the fact that your GP has referred you does not mean that the doctor at the hospital will automatically assess you and give you a solution to your problem. The first thing the doctor at the hospital will do is to gain your consent before your assessment. The doctor knows why your GP has referred you so why does he have to gain your consent before treatment?

My friend, it is the same principle. You have a will and a choice to choose Jesus. Other religions may force you to worship their God but God the Creator of heaven and earth has given every man a choice. You can choose to go to heaven and you can choose to go to hell. It is your choice.

3. I do not believe in hell because if God is so loving why will He create hell to punish people?

God has two sides. One side is so loving, so merciful and so forgiving but the other side of God is judgement. He is so loving that He sent His only son Jesus Christ to die for our sins.

For God so loved the world, that he gave his only begotten Son, that whosoever believeth in him should not perish, but have everlasting life.

John 3:16

He will also judge all those who do not accept this love and choose to remain in their sins and send them to hell.

For we must all appear before the judgment seat of Christ; that every one may receive the things done in his body, according to that he hath done, whether it be good or bad.
2 Corinthians 5:10

Even human beings are wise enough to create a place called prison for all those who commit various kinds of atrocities in this world and are considered too dangerous to live in society. In the same way that the world is able to condemn murderers to life imprisonment, God is also able to cast all those who continue in their sins into hell for eternal condemnation.

4. I pray every day.

Praying everyday does not save a person. There are so many gods in this world but there is only one God who is the Creator of heaven and earth. Only salvation will connect any human being to this God. Moreover, Jesus said that unless you are born again or saved, you cannot enter into the kingdom of God. He did not say "unless you pray you cannot enter into the kingdom of God." I announce to you Mr prayerful person, you need to be born again.

Jesus answered and said unto him, Verily, verily, I say unto thee, Except a man be born again, he cannot see the kingdom of God.

John 3:3

5. I go to church.

Going to church only makes you a church goer. It does not mean you are saved. God does not save people in groups. Salvation is an individual affair. Many people go to church and are in church but are not in Christ Jesus. Unless you are born again, your going to church will not save you. You can sing in the choir, be an usher, give offerings and even preach but if you are not born again, you cannot enter into the kingdom of God.

Jesus answered and said unto him, Verily, verily, I say unto thee, Except a man be born again, he cannot see the kingdom of God.

John 3:3

6. There is no God.

When I meet people and they say there is no God, I often wonder why any normal human being would think that way. When you look at the world and all that is in it, there must be someone who created it. Even if you think that the world came to being as a result of a big bang, who created that which the big bang came out of? If humans came into being as a result of evolution from a monkey to human who created the first monkey? If human beings came from a cave, who created the first cave? The same people who say they do not believe there is God believe in science and in nature. But who created both science and nature? It's amazing how human beings serve the creatures in the world instead of the Creator.

Who changed the truth of God into a lie, and worshipped and served the creature more than the Creator, who is blessed for ever. Amen.
                                              Romans 1:25

I do not understand these empty reasons that people give to say there is no God. If I tell you that no one created or made your mobile phone, you would say I am mad because you know that someone created it. If someone created or made a small mobile phone, then what about this whole big world? God must have created it. The Bible gives a good answer to all such people. A person who thinks there is no God is a fool. It is only a fool who will say there is no God.

The fool hath said in his heart, There is no God. They are corrupt, they have done abominable works, there is none that doeth good.

Psalm 14:1

When to Go

Fellow Christians, churches, body of Christ, pastors and fellow workers in the vineyard of The Most High God, the time to go is now!!! The time to win the lost at all cost is now. It cannot wait. Souls are perishing every second, every minute, every hour, every day, every month and every year. We must all roll up our sleeves and act now. Jesus told the disciples that the harvest is ready and we must go and win them. It is an emergency and the response to an emergency situation is now. When someone dials 999 to call for an ambulance, police or fire service, they must respond immediately. If they fail to respond quickly, it can mean someone's death. We are the ambulances, police and fire service personnel in the army of the Lord and we must head the call to GO now.

Jesus saith unto them, My meat is to do the will of him that sent me, and to finish his work.

Say not ye, There are yet four months, and then cometh harvest? behold, I say unto you, Lift up your eyes, and look on the fields; for they are white already to harvest.

John 4:34-35

Father in the name of Jesus, let signs and wonders follow me as I go and preach the gospel.

Confirm Your word by stretching forth Your hand to heal every form of sickness and diseases.

Stretch forth Your mighty hand and cast out devils and raise the dead.

Let Your people experience the power of the gospel in Jesus name. Amen

❧❦

Chapter 9

21 REASONS WHY WE MUST GO

The Lord has given each and every Christian the greatest commandment and commission to win the lost while on the earth. We must therefore aim to fulfil this Great Commission. We must heed the call and go to all nations with the gospel of Jesus Christ.

1. **We must go because it is the Great Commission.**

And Jesus came and spake unto them, saying, All power is given unto me in heaven and in earth.

Go ye therefore, and teach all nations, baptizing them in the name of the Father, and of the Son, and of the Holy Ghost:

Teaching them to observe all things whatsoever I have commanded you: and, lo, I am with you alway, even unto the end of the world. Amen.

Matthew 28:18-20

And he said unto them, Go ye into all the world, and preach the gospel to every creature.

He that believeth and is baptized shall be saved; but he that believeth not shall be damned.

Mark 16:15-16

2. We will be charged with murder if we refuse to fulfil the Great Commission.

The Lord considers us as murderers if we refuse to win the lost. We must take every opportunity we get to preach to any individual we meet. If we do not witness to them and they die in their sins, we are responsible for their final destination after life.

When I say unto the wicked, Thou shalt surely die; and thou givest him not warning, nor speakest to warn the wicked from his wicked way, to save his life; the same wicked man shall die in his iniquity; but his blood will I require at thine hand.

Ezekiel 3:18

3. God wants everyone saved, not just us and our families.

The majority of Christians are selfish about soul winning and they only want their families to be saved. But I want you to know that God wants every man to be saved. We must consciously extend the love of God to others. Everyone we meet is a candidate for heaven.

The Lord is not slack concerning his promise, as some men count slackness; but is longsuffering to us-ward, not willing that any should perish, but that all should come to repentance.

2 Peter 3:9

Who will have all men to be saved, and to come unto the knowledge of the truth.

1 Timothy 2:4

4. We must go because speaking the truth will set people free.

There are so many false religions out there but the truth is that Jesus is Christ is the only way to heaven. This is the truth that we have to preach otherwise many are going to perish in their sins. Many will sincerely perish in their sins having given their lives to the wrong god. When people get to know the truth, they are instantly freed from the bondage of false religions.

Jesus saith unto him, I am the way, the truth, and the life: no man cometh unto the Father, but by me.

John 14:6

And ye shall know the truth, and the truth shall make you free.

John 8:32

5. The church is the only institution that has been mandated by God to win the lost.

The main job of the church is to win the lost. The institutions of the world will not do this job for us. We have to be focused on the work God has given us to do and not deviate from it. It is not the main duty of the church to establish hospitals; that is the job of the Ministry of Health. It is not the main duty of the church to establish schools; that is the job of the Ministry of Education. The church is gradually losing its main vision of winning the lost and focusing on other things which are not its main aim. We must repent and go back to soul winning.

And all things are of God, who hath reconciled us to himself by Jesus Christ, and hath given to us the ministry of reconciliation;

To wit, that God was in Christ, reconciling the world unto himself, not imputing their trespasses unto them; and hath committed unto us the word of reconciliation.

2 Corinthians 5:18-19

6. We are created to do the good work of soul winning.

God created us to do good works and the greatest good work that He created us to do is soul winning.

For we are his workmanship, created in Christ Jesus unto good works, which God hath before ordained that we should walk in them.

Ephesians 2:10

7. Soul winning is our greatest opportunity to lay up treasures in heaven.

All the material things we acquire on this earth will be left behind when we die. You cannot go to heaven with your cars, houses and your possessions. But one thing is for sure, all the souls you win will go into your heavenly account. Blessed are they that die in the Lord as their works will follow them. Carry out the work of soul winning so you can lay up treasures in heaven.

And I heard a voice from heaven saying unto me, Write, Blessed are the dead which die in the Lord from henceforth: Yea, saith the Spirit, that they may rest from their labours; and their works do follow them.

Revelation 14:13

Lay not up for yourselves treasures upon earth, where moth and rust doth corrupt, and where thieves break through and steal:

But lay up for yourselves treasures in heaven, where neither moth nor rust doth corrupt, and where thieves do not break through nor steal:

Matthew 6:19-20

8. The person who win souls is a wise person.

A wise son or daughter will do that which pleases his or her father. Soul winning is the heartbeat of God, so if we want to please God the Father, we must carry out the work of soul winning.

The fruit of the righteous is a tree of life; and he that winneth souls is wise.

Proverbs 11:30

9. **We must win the lost because God loves the unsaved and He does not want them to perish in their sins.**

God loves mankind and He does not want anyone to die in their sins. He sent His only son Jesus Christ to come and die for us so that whosoever will believe in Him should not perish.

For God so loved the world, that he gave his only begotten Son, that whosoever believeth in him should not perish, but have everlasting life.

John 3:16

10. **God will make your life beautiful if you win souls.**

God is very interested in the soul winner. His heart is with those who care about the lost and He will bless them and make their lives beautiful.

And they that be wise shall shine as the brightness of the firmament; and they that turn many to righteousness as the stars for ever and ever.

Daniel 12:3

11. Soul winning is the heartbeat of God.

Soul winning is the reason why God became a man to save the world. Jesus, who is God, disrobed Himself of His Godly nature and became a man and died a shameful death on the cross to pay the penalty of our sins. He went through all this to ensure that all men will be saved. The Prince of Peace left His heavenly throne and glory to come to the earth to save us because soul winning is His heartbeat.

For the Son of man is come to seek and to save that which was lost.

Luke 19:10

12. We can see the signs of the end times.

The clock is ticking and we do not have enough time. We must move swiftly and carry out the work of soul winning because the end of the world is near. We cannot tell the exact day when the world will come to an end but Jesus gave us the signs of the end times. When you look around the world, you can see that almost all the signs of the end times that Jesus outlined in the scriptures are happening. This should make us sit up and win the lost before Jesus comes. There is no single day that you do not hear about conflicts, wars and killings in this world. It is a continuous thing that is happening all around us. Many people now love sin more than God. They have become very cold towards the gospel. So many false prophets have risen up and are preaching all sorts of messages. We do not have much time, we must act now.

And as he sat upon the mount of Olives, the disciples came unto him privately, saying, Tell us, when shall these things be? and what shall be the sign of thy coming, and of the end of the world?

And Jesus answered and said unto them, Take heed that no man deceive you.

For many shall come in my name, saying, I am Christ; and shall deceive many.

And ye shall hear of wars and rumours of wars: see that ye be not troubled: for all these things must come to pass, but the end is not yet.

For nation shall rise against nation, and kingdom against kingdom: and there shall be famines, and pestilences, and earthquakes, in divers places.

All these are the beginning of sorrows.

Then shall they deliver you up to be afflicted, and shall kill you: and ye shall be hated of all nations for my name's sake.

And then shall many be offended, and shall betray one another, and shall hate one another.

And many false prophets shall rise, and shall deceive many.

And because iniquity shall abound, the love of many shall wax cold.

Matthew 24:3-12

13. We must go because Christians have no other reason to exist than to make disciples.

There is no other reason why Christians are still alive today. You are still alive because God wants you to win souls. If you are not winning souls then God has a reason to exit you out of this world to heaven.

Every branch in me that beareth not fruit he taketh away: and every branch that beareth fruit, he purgeth it, that it may bring forth more fruit.

John 15:2

14. We must go because people must hear the gospel.

If we do not preach the gospel, the lost cannot hear it. If we do not preach the gospel, the lost cannot be saved. This is because if they cannot hear, they cannot be saved.

How then shall they call on him in whom they have not believed? and how shall they believe in him of whom they have not heard? and how shall they hear without a preacher?

Romans 10:14

15. Man has only one life to live.

I mentioned in the earlier chapters that no man will live forever. If you look around, you will notice that people die every day. The deaths of people are broadcasted everyday on the news. Ask yourself, where are all our forefathers? The answer is that they are all dead. Just as they are dead and gone, each and every human being will also die one day. Unfortunately, we do not know that day and so we must prepare ourselves for that important day. You may never know when the closest person to you is going to die. For it is appointed unto men once to die but after the death, there is judgement.

And as it is appointed unto men once to die, but after this the judgment:
                                                    Hebrews 9:27

16. We must go because we are ambassadors for Christ and the kingdom of heaven.

The Compact Oxford Dictionary and Thesaurus gives two very important definitions of an ambassador.

- An ambassador is a person sent by a state as its permanent representative in a foreign country.

- An ambassador is a person who represents or promotes a particular activity.

A Christian is therefore an ambassador who represents Jesus Christ and the kingdom of heaven to promote the activities of soul winning. We represent

God the Father in a different country called earth and we must not forget why we are here. We are heavenly citizens and we must carry out the vision of heaven on earth.

Now then we are ambassadors for Christ, as though God did beseech you by us: we pray you in Christ's stead, be ye reconciled to God.

2 Corinthians 5:20

17. We must go because the harvest is ready.

We must avoid procrastination and overcome any excuses and obstacles to soul winning. The harvest is ready and all the work has been done for us. The Lord has made the world ready by dying on the cross for the sins of mankind. We do not have any excuse and the time is now. Christians are so lazy and reluctant to carry out this great work. This is because the enemy, who wants mankind to go to hell, is working tirelessly behind the scenes to prevent us from going. May the Lord open your eyes as you read this book, to see how large the harvest is and how ready it is. Our harvest field is the world and it is ready and crying for help. There is a cry from Macedonia, there is a cry from Africa, there is a cry from Europe and there is a cry from Asia. Let us go and win the lost at all cost.

And a vision appeared to Paul in the night; There stood a man of Macedonia, and prayed him, saying, Come over into Macedonia, and help us.

And after he had seen the vision, immediately we endeavoured to go into Macedonia, assuredly gathering that the Lord had called us for to preach the gospel unto them.

Acts 16:9-10

18. We must go to prove that we are not ashamed of Jesus.

In order to prove that you are not ashamed of Jesus Christ, we must go and preach the gospel to every creature. Some people are ashamed of their salvation. They are Christians but do not want anyone to know that they are Christians. These kind of Christians are ashamed of God and cannot profess the gospel in front of others. But we must be warned. Jesus said if we are ashamed of Him before others, He will also be ashamed of us. We must therefore heed this warning and propagate the gospel of Jesus Christ.

For whosoever shall be ashamed of me and of my words, of him shall the Son of man be ashamed, when he shall come in his own glory, and in his Father's, and of the holy angels.

Luke 9:26

19. We must go to prove that we are true Christians.

If you are truly saved, you will not want to hide your Christianity. You will broadcast it everywhere you go. When you are given a nice gift, do you keep to yourself or do you tell your friends about it? In the same way, that when we receive something good we broadcast it, we must also broadcast the Lord to others. Real Christians bring forth other Christians into the kingdom of God. We must let our light shine before others. A light cannot be kept in darkness and we must let others know about Jesus by preaching the gospel to them.

Ye are the light of the world. A city that is set on an hill cannot be hid.

Neither do men light a candle, and put it under a bushel, but on a candlestick; and it giveth light unto all that are in the house.

Let your light so shine before men, that they may see your good works, and glorify your Father which is in heaven.

Matthew 5:14-16

Wherever you worship, ensure that you have other Christians in the church that you personally led to Christ. When you sit in the church and you look around you and realise that you have not personally brought anyone to that church, then there is something wrong with your Christian life. This is because if you are a real Christian, you will bring others to Christ.

And other sheep I have, which are not of this fold: them also I must bring, and they shall hear my voice; and there shall be one fold, and one shepherd.

John 10:16

20. We must go to add ourselves to the few labourers.

Although the harvest is ready, only few people are willing to go. When you go to church, look around and you will notice that only a few people go for evangelism. Most Christians do not care whether people go to hell or not. Be among the few labourers who are willing to work for the Lord. Be among those few labourers who have the zeal to win the lost at all cost.

Therefore said he unto them, The harvest truly is great, but the labourers are few: pray ye therefore the Lord of the harvest, that he would send forth labourers into his harvest.

Luke 10:2

21. We must go to bring forth fruit.

The Lord expects all His children to bring forth fruit. He has ordained us to go and preach to the lost and ensure that they stay in His kingdom. In order to bear fruit in the kingdom of God, we must ensure that others convert and give their lives to Jesus. This is the fruit that Jesus was talking about in the passage of scripture below.

Ye have not chosen me, but I have chosen you, and ordained you, that ye should go and bring forth fruit, and that your fruit should remain: that whatsoever ye shall ask of the Father in my name, he may give it you.

John 15:16

Lord Jesus, I ask you for the grace to follow-up souls that have been won into Your kingdom.
Give me the wisdom to teach and establish the new converts in Your house.
Equip me oh Lord to train and bring up the newborn believer in the fear of the Lord. Thank you Jesus for answering my prayer. Amen

ॐॐ

Chapter 10

SOUL WINNING AND FOLLOW-UP

Follow-up is a very important aspect of soul winning. Without it, the work of the soul winner will be in vain. This is because follow-up is what establishes the soul in the kingdom of God or in the house of God. When a soul is saved, the soul is like a newborn baby and has to be helped to grow up in the Lord. The process of growing up in the Lord starts with follow-up after the soul has been won. The main work involved in soul winning actually starts after the soul has been won.

In the natural, when a baby is born, the parents take care of the baby right from infancy to adulthood. In the spirit, when a person gives his or her life to

Jesus, a new spiritual baby has been born. This baby has to be taken care of by the soul winner or the pastor for the newborn baby to pass through the infant stage and childhood stage and become an adult Christian. When a Christian is a baby Christian, they exhibit similar characteristics as a baby in the natural realm. The Christian does not go to church regularly, does not read the Bible all the time, does not pray everyday and does not even know how to pray. The baby Christian may even fall several times after they are saved and they will need counselling and encouragement to stand firm in the Lord.

The baby Christian will not yet fully understand what has taken place in their lives by accepting Jesus Christ as their Lord and Saviour. They need to be taught the basics of Christianity and other important topics that will contribute to their establishment in Christ. Some Christians remain baby Christians for many years because they had no one to follow them up. I advise every soul winner to do follow-up after winning the souls. I advise my church members to follow-up the souls they win for Christ as well as the people they invite to church. Although the church does its own follow-up, the souls are often more comfortable with the people who won them for Christ. Therefore, I advise all those who win souls to follow-up the souls they have won themselves. Follow-up involves

praying for the new converts, visiting and phone calls
and counselling and teaching the new converts.

FOLLOW-UP THROUGH PRAYERS

1. **Pray that the new convert will be established
   in Christ and planted in the Kingdom and
   the House of God.**

*Those that be planted in the house of the LORD shall
flourish in the courts of our God.*

Psalm 92:13

*As ye have therefore received Christ Jesus the Lord, so
walk ye in him:*

*Rooted and built up in him, and stablished in the
faith, as ye have been taught, abounding therein with
thanksgiving.*

Colossians 2:6-7

2. **Pray that Christ will be formed in the
   newborn Christian.**

*My little children, of whom I travail in birth again
until Christ be formed in you,*

Galatians 4:19

3. Pray for God to open the eyes of the newborn Christian to understand His word.

Open thou mine eyes, that I may behold wondrous things out of thy law.

Psalm 119:18

The eyes of your understanding being enlightened; that ye may know what is the hope of his calling, and what the riches of the glory of his inheritance in the saints,

Ephesians 1:18

4. Pray that God's will be done in the newborn Christian's life.

Thy kingdom come. Thy will be done in earth, as it is in heaven.

Matthew 6:10

5. Pray that God will give the new convert the spirit of wisdom and revelation in the knowledge of Him.

Wherefore I also, after I heard of your faith in the Lord Jesus, and love unto all the saints,

Cease not to give thanks for you, making mention of you in my prayers;

That the God of our Lord Jesus Christ, the Father of glory, may give unto you the spirit of wisdom and revelation in the knowledge of him:

Ephesians 1:15-17

6. Pray that God will fill the new convert with the knowledge of His will.

For this cause we also, since the day we heard it, do not cease to pray for you, and to desire that ye might be filled with the knowledge of his will in all wisdom and spiritual understanding;

Colossians 1:9

7. Pray that the new convert will love God's work.

For we are his workmanship, created in Christ Jesus unto good works, which God hath before ordained that we should walk in them.

Ephesians 2:10

8. Pray that the new convert will bear fruit in the kingdom of God.

Ye have not chosen me, but I have chosen you, and ordained you, that ye should go and bring forth fruit, and that your fruit should remain: that whatsoever ye shall ask of the Father in my name, he may give it you.

John 15:16

FOLLOW-UP THROUGH VISITATION AND PHONE CALLS

Sometimes you will have to visit the newborn converts in order to encourage them to come to church. I once visited a new convert who did not want to come to church. The excuse he gave was that he had not had his bath nor ironed his clothes. So I asked him to go and have his bath while I ironed for him. After bathing, he dressed up and I took him to church. New converts come up with all sorts of excuses in other not to fellowship regularly. But this is because they are baby Christians and they must be encouraged to serve God. At the initial stages of their conversion, you may have to literally pick them up to attend church until they become stable.

Not forsaking the assembling of ourselves together, as the manner of some is; but exhorting one another: and so much the more, as ye see the day approaching.

Hebrews 10:25

Sometimes, you have to follow up with phone calls to check the state of the new converts. This works especially when the new convert does not want you to visit because of certain conditions in the house. You must respect this and use the method of phone calls.

FOLLOW-UP THROUGH COUNSELLING OR TEACHING OF THE WORD

The preaching of the word of God to the new convert is of paramount importance as far as follow-up is concerned. The newborn baby can only grow by the word of God. They cannot grow by eating physical food but by eating spiritual food which is the word of God. Just as a newborn baby needs milk in the natural to grow, the new born again Christian also needs spiritual milk which is the word of God to grow.

As newborn babes, desire the sincere milk of the word, that ye may grow thereby:

1 Peter 2:2

Teach the new convert the basics of Christian living so that he or she can build upon it. Use the word of God to counsel them.

Teach the new born Christian about the following aspects of being a born again Christian:

- *Understanding Salvation*
- *Understanding Water Baptism*
- *Holy Ghost Baptism*
- *Fellowship or Going to Church*
- *Prayer*
- *Fasting*
- *Witnessing or Soul Winning*
- *Giving to support the kingdom of God*

❧

Chapter 11

WHAT DO YOU WORSHIP?

What you choose to worship as your god is very significant. I once watched a clip of a lady who said she had to memorise the names of over 2,000 gods. What an incredible number of different gods catering for different needs! I am grateful I have one Almighty, All-Sufficient God who is exceedingly, abundantly able to do more than I could ask or ever hope for. I once spoke to a lady who informed me that she fed her god every morning. I then asked, "where is your god?" She replied, "in my small room." So I asked "how can your god live in just a small part of your house and why do you feed your god instead of him feeding you?" This lady could not give me an answer. You see, my God feeds me and provides for all my needs. One day, I saw a god displayed in a man's car. I wondered, "how can you carry your god around? Surely, your god is supposed to carry you and not the other way round?" My mighty God protects me and bears me in His everlasting arms.

Amazingly, none of these gods produced an answer for their followers. Yet you see millions of people, both educated and uneducated, wasting their time worshipping objects carved by men. These objects are kept in shrines, homes and even cars for people to carry around and worship them.

God is not an object made with hands

Millions of people worship objects made of gold, silver, stone and even wood. They carve these objects into shapes and bow down to things that they have made with their own hands. These objects have eyes yet cannot see. They have ears yet cannot hear. They have mouths yet cannot speak. They have noses yet cannot smell. They have arms yet cannot lift. They even have legs yet they cannot walk. Instead, it is the very people who worship these so-called idols or gods who perform these activities for their god. In short, these are deaf and dumb idols. My Bishop once told a story about one of his pastors who went to visit a village. Whilst he was approaching the village, he suddenly realised he needed to urinate. He saw an area just off the footpath, by a large stone, and decided that was a suitable spot. As he started, he heard a loud commotion. Alarmed, he looked up and saw a crowd approaching him and shouting; "stop urinating on our god, stop urinating on our god!" The large stone was the god of the villagers. This god is an example of a deaf and dumb idol. It could not speak for itself, even just to tell the pastor to stop urinating on him. It was totally silent. The word of God describes these deaf and dumb idols in the following scriptures.

Their idols are silver and gold, the work of men's hands.

They have mouths, but they speak not: eyes have they, but they see not:

They have ears, but they hear not: noses have they, but they smell not:

They have hands, but they handle not: feet have they, but they walk not: neither speak they through their throat.

They that make them are like unto them; so is every one that trusteth in them.

Psalm 115:4-8

*Hear ye the word which the LORD speaketh unto you,
O house of Israel:*

*Thus saith   the LORD, Learn not the way of the
heathen, and be not dismayed at the signs of heaven;
for the heathen are dismayed at them.*

*For the customs of the people are vain: for one cutteth
a tree out of the forest, the work of the hands of the
workman, with the axe.*

*They deck it with silver and with gold; they fasten it
with nails and with hammers, that it move not.*

*They are upright as the palm tree, but speak not: they
must needs be borne, because they cannot go. Be not
afraid of them; for they cannot do evil, neither also is
it in them to do good.*

*Forasmuch as there is none like unto thee, O LORD;
thou art great, and thy name is great in might.*

*Who would not fear thee, O King of nations? for to
thee doth it appertain: forasmuch as among all the
wise men of the nations, and in all their kingdoms,
there is none like unto thee.*

But they are altogether brutish and foolish: the stock is a doctrine of vanities.

Silver spread into plates is brought from Tarshish, and gold from Uphaz, the work of the workman, and of the hands of the founder: blue and purple is their clothing: they are all the work of cunning men.

But the LORD is the true God, he is the living God, and an everlasting king: at his wrath the earth shall tremble, and the nations shall not be able to abide his indignation.

Thus shall ye say unto them, The gods that have not made the heavens and the earth, even they shall perish from the earth, and from under these heavens.

Jeremiah 10:1-11

What profiteth the graven image that the maker thereof hath graven it; the molten image, and a teacher of lies, that the maker of his work trusteth therein, to make dumb idols?

Woe unto him that saith to the wood, Awake; to the dumb stone, Arise, it shall teach! Behold, it is laid over with gold and silver, and there is no breath at all in the midst of it.

Habakkuk 2:18-19

God is not an animal

Some religions consider animals as god and they bow down to these animals which are created for us to eat. God the Creator of the heavens and the earth is not an animal. How can a human being created in the very image of the Most High God bow down to animals that God has given man dominion over? How can creatures such as cows, snakes, pigs, tigers, elephants, monkeys, wolves, dogs, goats and horses be worshipped in His place?

And God said, Let us make man in our image, after our likeness: and let them have dominion over the fish of the sea, and over the fowl of the air, and over the cattle, and over all the earth, and over every creeping thing that creepeth upon the earth.

Genesis 1:26

The Almighty God created human beings to be superior to animals. To see humans worshipping animals means mankind has indeed lowered itself and made animals more superior than themselves. God put mankind in charge of animals, not the other way round. This is ignorance to the fullest extent. Mankind has reached this state because they have refused to recognise the Creator of the heavens and the earth as God. The verse of scripture below explains it all.

Because that, when they knew God, they glorified him not as God, neither were thankful; but became vain in their imaginations, and their foolish heart was darkened.

Professing themselves to be wise, they became fools, And changed the glory of the uncorruptible God into an image made like to corruptible man, and to birds, and fourfooted beasts, and creeping things.

Romans 1:21-24

A darkened heart and mind is hostile to God and such a person will serve anything, regardless of whether they are educated or not.

God is not a man

Some religions actually worship men and this is not right. When you worship a man, that man becomes your idol. We must understand that God is not an imperfect human being, neither is He an icon or a figurehead. The Bible tells us that God is not a man and God cannot lie.

God is not a man, that he should lie; neither the son of man, that he should repent: hath he said, and shall he not do it? or hath he spoken, and shall he not make it good?

Numbers 23:19

Men lie all the time. We cannot even take care of ourselves, let alone be worshipped as god. Men change all the time but God can never change. A man will say to a lady "I love you and I want to marry you" and later change his mind and break that lady's heart.

How can such a person who is not morally correct be your god? It is simple, a man cannot be your god! In fact, one of the main reasons why a man cannot be your god is that he does not even know when he will die. Today he is alive but tomorrow he is dead. Job chapter 14 explains that even a tree has more hope than a man because it can regrow after being cut down.

Man that is born of a woman is of few days, and full of trouble.

He cometh forth like a flower, and is cut down: he fleeth also as a shadow, and continueth not.

And dost thou open thine eyes upon such an one, and bringest me into judgment with thee?

Who can bring a clean thing out of an unclean? not one.

Seeing his days are determined, the number of his months are with thee, thou hast appointed his bounds that he cannot pass;

Turn from him, that he may rest, till he shall accomplish, as an hireling, his day.

For there is hope of a tree, if it be cut down, that it will sprout again, and that the tender branch thereof will not cease.

Though the root thereof wax old in the earth, and the stock thereof die in the ground;

Yet through the scent of water it will bud, and bring forth boughs like a plant.

But man dieth, and wasteth away: yea, man giveth up the ghost, and where is he?

Job 14:1-10

God is a Spirit

Do not be deceived by the many definitions men have given to God! Many have perceived the Creator to be a man, an animal, a stone and even trees. But these definitions are completely wrong. God is none of these helpless, inferior things. The word of God gives a classic definition of God. Almighty God is a Spirit.

God is a Spirit: and they that worship him must worship him in spirit and in truth.

John 4:24

The above passage of scripture in John 4:24 puts God in the right perspective. God is a Spirit. He neither has beginning nor end. He himself is the beginning and the end. No one created God because He Himself is existence. He cannot be compared to any kind of god. There is only one God and aside Him is no other god. All others are liars. Any human who claim to be Almighty God is a liar.

Unto thee it was shewed, that thou mightest know that the LORD he is God; there is none else beside him.

Deuteronomy 4:35

ॐ≪ॐ

Chapter 12

HOW CAN I RECEIVE SALVATION?

For God so loved the world that He sent His only son Jesus that whosoever believes in Him should not perish but have everlasting life. God has already paid the price for you by sacrificing a life for you. This life is the life of Jesus which has been sacrificed for you for eternity. In actual fact, Jesus bought you from Satan with His life and Satan does not have the right to take you to hell.

For God so loved the world, that he gave his only begotten Son, that whosoever believeth in him should not perish, but have everlasting life.

John 3:16

The truth is that you cannot be saved by your own works.

For by grace are ye saved through faith; and that not of yourselves: it is the gift of God.

Ephesians 2:8-9

In fact, all our good deeds are like filthy rags before the Lord.

But we are all as an unclean thing, and all our righteousnesses are as filthy rags; and we all do fade as a leaf; and our iniquities, like the wind, have taken us away.

Isaiah 64:6

You can be very loving, you can be so kind, you can give all your money to the poor, you can establish many charities to help mankind, you can pay your tithe, sing in the choir and even preach but all these cannot save you. There is no such thing as "I am too good to go hell." I have often heard people say that I am a good person and therefore I will go to heaven. But be not deceived, you can never be good enough for heaven. It is not by our own works but by the mercy and love of God.

Not by works of righteousness which we have done, but according to his mercy he saved us, by the washing

of regeneration, and renewing of the Holy Ghost.
Titus 3:5

There is only one way to get saved and that is through Jesus Christ. All others are liars. Jesus said, *"I am the way, the truth and the life, no man comes to the father but by Me."*

Jesus saith unto him, I am the way, the truth, and the life: no man cometh unto the Father, but by me.
John 14:6

Jesus also said that He is the door to heaven.

Then said Jesus unto them again, Verily, verily, I say unto you, I am the door of the sheep.
John 10:7

Even the very door to heaven is Jesus. My friend do not be deceived by the doctrine of devils being preached by some prominent people you know because one day they will all bow before the king of kings and the Lord of Lords. The word of God tells us clearly that there is no other name under heaven whereby we must be saved. In other words, there is no salvation in any other name except Jesus.

Neither is there salvation in any other: for there is none other name under heaven given among men, whereby we must be saved.

$\qquad$ *Acts 4:12*

The word of God also tells us that whosoever shall call on the name of the Lord shall be saved.

And it shall come to pass, that whosoever shall call on the name of the Lord shall be saved.

$\qquad$ *Acts 2:21*

For there is no difference between the Jew and the Greek: for the same Lord over all is rich unto all that call upon him.

For whosoever shall call upon the name of the Lord shall be saved.

$\qquad$ *Romans 10:12-13*

Whosoever means "whosoever." It does not matter how deep your sins are, the blood of Jesus can wash it away. There is no sin that God cannot forgive; there is no sin under heaven that the blood of Jesus cannot wash. It is only up to you the individual to acknowledge that you are a sinner and repent of your sins. Repentance is of the heart. That is why Jesus said that, unless a man is born again he cannot see the Kingdom of God. Except a man is born of the water which is the word, and of the Spirit, he cannot enter into the kingdom of God.

Jesus answered and said unto him, Verily, verily, I say unto thee, Except a man be born again, he cannot see the kingdom of God.

John 3:3-5

When you become born again or saved, God gives you a new heart. Your heart is created again and you become a new person. All your sins are washed away by the precious blood of Jesus. You become a new creature and you can no longer be condemned by your past. Jesus makes everything new.

Therefore if any man be in Christ, he is a new creature: old things are passed away; behold, all things are become new.

2 Corinthians 5:17

As soon as you receive Jesus into your life, you are translated from the kingdom of darkness which is the devil's kingdom, into the kingdom of light which is God's kingdom. The Lord gives you power to become His son or daughter.

Who hath delivered us from the power of darkness, and hath translated us into the kingdom of his dear Son:

Colossians 1:13

But as many as received him, to them gave he power to become the sons of God, even to them that believe on his name:

John 1:12

You are suddenly adopted into the family of God. Hallelujah! Amen! Now, if you will confess Jesus with your mouth and believe that God has raised Him from the dead, you shall be saved.

That if thou shalt confess with thy mouth the Lord Jesus, and shalt believe in thine heart that God hath raised him from the dead, thou shalt be saved.

Romans 10:9-10

You must believe with your heart and confess with your mouth that Jesus is Lord.

PRAYER OF SALVATION

If you are ready to surrender your life to Jesus, please say this prayer.

My Father in heaven, I recognise that I am a sinner.
I recognise that the Lord Jesus died for me and paid the penalty for my sins.

Dear Lord, today I repent of my sins and I accept Jesus Christ as my Lord and Saviour. Wash me with your blood and make me holy.

Please write my name in the book of life and give me the grace to serve you.
Thank you that I am born again.
Amen

Other Books by Rev. Ernest Addo

Three Dimensions of Man

The Foundations of True Faith

The Father's Love

Meeting and Knowing the Holy Spirit

How to Pray: 60 Minutes in His Presence

To order copies or for more information,
please contact ernest.addo1@yahoo.com.